Reversing the
Ostrich Approach to Diversity:
Pulling your head out of the sand.

Five simple concepts you can use now
to reap bottom-line results
by honoring diversity.

Reversing the Ostrich Approach to Diversity:
Pulling your head out of the sand.

**Five simple concepts you can use now
to reap bottom-line results
by honoring diversity.**

A. S. Tolbert, Ph.D.

First Edition

Nasus
Publishing
Minneapolis, Minnesota

Reversing the Ostrich Approach to Diversity:
Pulling your head out of the sand.

Five simple concepts you can use now to reap bottom-line
results by honoring diversity.

A. S. Tolbert, Ph.D.

Artwork © John Bush, Minneapolis, MN

Special thanks go to Humorist Joe Lovitt, and the collaborative
writing efforts of Ray Myers and Armida Mendez-Russell.

Published by:
Nasus Publishing
1509 Irving Lane
Minneapolis, MN 55337
www.successideas.com

First Printing 2002
Printed in the United States of America

Publisher's Cataloging-in-Publication
(Provided by Quality Books, Inc.)

Tolbert, A.S.
     Reversing the ostrich approach to diversity : pulling
your head out of the sand : five simple concepts you can
use now to reap bottom-line results by honoring
diversity / A.S. Tolbert. -- 1st ed.
     p. cm.
     Includes bibliographical references.
     LCCN 2001099831
     ISBN 0-9670291-3-9

     1. Diversity in the workplace. I. Title.

HF5549.5.M5T65 2002   658.3'008
                        QBI02-200092

Contents

Chapter 4

Chapter 5

Chapter 6

Foreword

I remember one company executive who said to me, "Julie, I just don't have time to do the 'personal diversity work' that you and others think is the right thing to do. Just tell me what to do. Give me the one-pager on diversity!" It was said, not with resistance, but with reality — the reality of so many things to do and so little time.

That short conversation impacted me greatly. For the first time, I felt empathy for people I previously labeled as those who just didn't get it and who, I thought, were looking for a way out of dealing with diversity. But, that wasn't true – they just wanted clear, direct guidelines on what to do. Ever since, I've worked hard to offer practical, workable suggestions.

Reversing the Ostrich Approach to Diversity: Pulling your head out of the sand has much more substance than a "one-pager," yet it accomplishes what that executive wanted. While it's researched-based, it gives clear examples of specific diversity issues and then tells us what to do in a simple, direct way. And the humor works well. Because of the "eggshell dilemma," which Amy describes in Chapter 2, we have become afraid of telling jokes or adding humor of any kind when we talk about diversity. I'm glad that Amy has had the courage to address the seriousness of this topic and also show us that humor and diversity can be used in the same sentence.

Amy addresses an area that I have found especially helpful to people in organizations – knowing the right words to use. As a diversity consultant I get a lot of grief from people about "political correctness." Yet, I push on about using appropriate language. I have found that when people know their language is appropriate, they converse more. And when we converse more, we learn more, we understand each other, and we grow in our appreciation of each other. All these behaviors help us live and work in a changing world. And, I find the tips and exercises she provides at the end of chapters two through six — Pull Your Head Out of the Sand — especially useful, even if your head isn't in the sand.

I met Amy when I was introduced to the *Discovering Diversity Profile*®, which she co-authored several years ago. I've found that instrument especially helpful for getting clarity on what diversity is and gaining insight on our individual levels of understanding and behaviors of diversity. It helps simplify the complex topic of diversity. This book does the same.

Once people internalize and appreciate the wisdom provided in this book, they will feel more comfortable with diversity and be ready to tackle more of the 'personal diversity work' that I believe we all need to do on an ongoing basis.

Have fun reading this book!

Julie O'Mara
Co-author, *Managing Workforce 2000: Gaining the Diversity Advantage*
Author, *Diversity Activities and Training Designs*
CEO, O'Mara and Associates
Castro Valley, California

Chapter 1

The Ostrich, the Sand, and You: What's the diversity connection?

What does diversity have to do with an ostrich? Consider this definition from the American Heritage Dictionary:

os·trich (ŏs/trĭch, ôs/-) *n.*, *pl.* **ostrich** or **os·trich·es**. 1.a. A large, swift-running flightless bird (Struthio camelus) of Africa, characterized by a long bare neck, small head, and two-toed feet. It is the largest living bird. b. A rhea. **2. One who tries to avoid disagreeable situations by refusing to face them.**

Hm-m-m. So, our dear struthio camelus can run its tail feathers off and flap 'til it flops but, alas, can never take flight. Well, when it comes to diversity issues, neither can we. All the running, hiding and avoidance (a.k.a. the ostrich approach) won't change what's going on around us. And while the image of an ostrich burying its head in the sand is based on myth rather than fact, it is the perfect icon to depict the many avoidance tactics we use to deal with the tough stuff. The tough issues won't go away just because we refuse to look at them.

Yet, dealing with diversity challenges doesn't have to be painful. And it doesn't have to take weeks out of your already over-stuffed schedule. This book simplifies some of the complex concepts of diversity work to make them immediately applicable in your day-to-day life. In the following pages you'll find basic, to-the-point information followed by do-it-now action steps that can quickly set the wheels of change in motion. It's the kind of change that also brings an opportunity to positively impact relationships, productivity, and profits. Who couldn't use a little more of that?

Here is a brief description of each of the five simple concepts you'll be exploring in the following chapters:

1 *Stop Walking On Eggshells: Define and use positive confrontation.* Relationships are built, and you can influence how they are developed and shaped. Yet, there is often a lot of energy-draining, stutter-stepping going on that hinders relationship development with those of different cultures or abilities. You can stop walking on eggshells by taking risks, appropriately confronting difficult situations, and managing conflict. Once you do, you will benefit from strong, healthy relationships that can help you reach both personal and professional goals.

2 *I'm Okay, But "They" Need Help: Why should I change?* There are rewards for implementing personal change. However, change is unlikely without identifying those benefits and making a conscious choice to implement the changes needed to acquire them. You'll learn about and use the head, heart, and hand model to help make you more aware of the things you say and do. This model emphasizes that, in every situation, you choose your response. By recognizing your ability to change outcomes by making different response choices, you can begin to experience the benefits of those changes.

3 *Help Others Matter: Unleash the power of diversity.* You are either included or excluded by others, which causes you to feel and behave in certain ways. You also include or exclude others. Individuals who feel they are being

excluded often respond with less motivation and productivity. You have the power to change that response by choosing words and actions that make them feel they matter.

4   *Broaden Your World View: See things as they are not as you are.* All of us have biases, prejudices, and stereotypical ideas of others; we are all ethnocentric. It's part of being human. However, not admitting to these negative social forces damages your relationships with others, the bottom line, and your potential to advance along your career path.

5   *Which Way Out of the Desert: Progress is made with just one step.* Take one tiny step forward. Take another. How about one more? Before long you'll discover you're a long way from where you started. When it comes to making changes the important thing is to just start. Risk-taking and moving into discomfort will move you away from a limiting view of the world and toward a broader, more enriching one. The goal is to overcome unconscious acts of exclusion and build more effective relationships.

Did you notice the key theme threaded throughout each of these concepts? Relationships ... how you choose to live, play, and work with others.

You can develop and build upon your relationships in a diverse environment by applying the five simple concepts outlined above. While the five concepts are simple, the application of them to your own life will take some effort. To make this easier, each concept is supported with illustrations, quotes, and a chapter summary that includes suggestions for immediate action that you can take. You will be asked to observe, reflect, listen, make choices, lean into discomfort, and openly communicate over and over again, with slightly different purposes depending on the chapter content. Begin with the ones that feel most comfortable or make the most sense to you. The objective is to simply begin navigating through the world with more awareness and a broader perspective.

Why Is Navigating Through a Diverse World So Important?

The short answer is: because the world is changing, including your little corner of it.

With the fast-paced changes facing each of us, the corporate sector, and the world, diversity and globalization issues are even more crucial to the success and survival of individuals, families, and businesses. Shifting expectations, differences impacting our day-to-day lives, and our shrinking world, all provide daunting challenges to us personally. Changing demographics, global competition, worker productivity, market niche focus, and employee recruitment and retention, all provide daunting challenges to organizations.

The good news is that these challenges also provide unique opportunities to the proactive, strategic-minded, diversity-aware individual and organization. These personal and professional advantages can — and should — be yours.

What Makes Us Diverse?

Our culture ... the various subcultures to which we belong. To function effectively, we must understand culture and its impact on us. Our challenge is to learn about difference, appreciate that it brings uniqueness, and work effectively with those differences in creating a win/win outcome. Managing diversity is a critical component for building effective relationships with others.

You can choose to view the process of learning about others and their differences as being either overwhelming or exciting. The rewards will be far greater when viewing it with excitement and anticipation. By developing an understanding of others, your personal gains include:

- Freedom to express your opinions and thoughts in a safe environment
- An increase in your contributions and value to self and others
- Reduced stress associated with marginalization (being excluded)
- A heightened sense of belonging

- A much fuller and richer picture of the world — as though you're using a new set of eyes and ears
- The creation of long-standing, trusting relationships
- Improved ability to bring your talents and skills — your full self — to life.

Benefits of addressing diversity and change issues for the organization include:

- Reducing costs associated with marginalization of employees and lower productivity
- Creating a competitive market presence in the global arena
- Attracting and retaining the best employees
- Gaining a marketing advantage through enhanced customer service, product development, and innovation
- Increasing employee productivity, creativity, quality, and teamwork
- Fostering an organizational climate that honors each individual's contribution
- Enhancing public image.

Diversity work is change work. Yet it doesn't have to be difficult work; it can be exhilarating, enlightening, and ever-evolving as you begin to experience the powerful advantages of honoring diversity in your life. Honoring others occurs when you internalize the lessons and find *personal value* in a diverse environment.

The information presented in this book is not intended to be a complete or all-encompassing answer to the complexities of diversity education. Instead, it is direct information and action steps that will take you on an adventurous journey out of the desolate, mirage-ridden desert of misperception that the dear ostrich calls home.

You have the power to broaden your own perception and define expectations based on facts, not fiction. All you need to do is steady your stance, firmly plant your feet on the ground, and gently *pull, Pull, PULL* your head out of the sand.

To give you a quick start with some of the end of chapter exercises, I've posted a few detailed worksheets in PDF format on my Web site at:

www.ECCOInternational.com

Please feel free to download and use them with this book.

Chapter 2

Stop Walking on Eggshells: Define and use "good" confrontation

"When people rage, it's because they don't have the courage to give their true emotions a voice."

Dr. Phil McGraw
Psychologist, author

The Eggshell Dilemma

What Is Walking on Eggshells?

Walking on eggshells is *avoiding any situation that might result in confrontation or hurting someone's feelings.* Walking on eggshells can occur when we:

- Tiptoe around or avoid sensitive issues and allow resentment and misunderstandings to pile up

- Make inappropriate assumptions, or hold on to false stereotypes, about others

- Worry obsessively about offending someone or saying the wrong thing

- Fear lawsuits or getting the organization into trouble by violating hostile work environment, EEO or Affirmative Action policies
- Fear personal harm — the term "going postal" is universally understood as a potential outcome for workplace conflicts
- Don't want to embarrass ourselves
- Repress emotions or resentments that build up and seep out sideways at innocent bystanders.

Join the Eggshell Club!

Given the physical workout most employees get every day on the job, you wonder why it is that some businesses include health club memberships as part of the benefits they offer to employees! Here are some common workplace exercises:

- *The Neck Stretch-and-Crane* — Peer over the cubicle wall or around the corner at the other employees. Sum up how they're different from you. If detected, snap neck back into position.
- *The Sideways Leer* — Without turning your head or neck, arch your eyebrows and pop your eyes half way out of their sockets sideways trying to see how other employees are doing their jobs differently from you.

- *The Defensive Backpedal* — If confronted for being insensitive to the beliefs, ideals, appearance, or work styles of others, trot backwards with your arms extended in front of you while claiming you "meant nothing by it."

- *The Offensive Frontpedal* — In the same situation, barrel forward while telling your accuser, "That's the way I am. If you don't like it, that's YOUR problem!"

And our old favorite ...

- *The Eggshell Walk* — When working with anyone whose skin tone, hair, gender, sexual orientation, nationality, ability, religious belief, age, body type, wardrobe, car, musical preference (I'm getting petty here, but you get the idea) are different from yours, gingerly and silently tiptoe around any issues you may have with them. If they have problems with you, raise your knees a little higher, step a little lighter, and dart sideways to avoid any confrontation.

With so much exercise going on, it's a wonder there are so many people out of shape in the world. But it's also not surprising that there's as much conflict in the workplace as there is today.

We use *walking on eggshells* as a coping mechanism to avoid conflict when working with people different from ourselves. Open lines of communication transform eggshells into solid rock pathways.

Managing Conflict

Ever watch a TV newscast and see robbery suspects being taken into custody? They usually hide beneath a coat, turn from the cameras, and sink into the backseat of the squad car as if trying to become part of the upholstery. A robbery suspect seldom gazes proudly into the camera and admits, "Sure, I robbed the bank! But it was necessary to achieve my goal of financial independence!"

> *"There is such a thing as a man being too proud to fight."*
> Woodrow Wilson
> 28th U.S. President

Negative conflict can occur even when the best of intentions drives behaviors. We typically react to questionable behaviors (robbery), not intentions (financial independence).

The less we know about the people with whom we work, the more potential there is for misinterpreting behavior and its impact. We may not know that we "push the buttons" of other people, but, nonetheless, we DO push them, just like other people push our buttons without knowing it.

The simple resolution to conflict management is to communicate openly in our interactions in areas such as language, style, expectations, and commonalties.

Removing the Mask of Diplomacy

Diplomacy can be defined as *the art of making others believe that you believe what you don't believe.* If that's correct, it might explain why so few of us are diplomats. Our behaviors usually reflect what we believe to be true, no matter what we say otherwise. That's why we run into problems if our actions communicate one idea and our explanations for those actions seem to say something entirely different.

> *"A diplomat is a person who can tell you to go to hell in such a way that you actually look forward to the trip."*
>
> Caskie Stinnett
> U.S. American writer

The trick is to match behavior with words. Walk the talk. If we spent our time adapting our behavior instead of trying to prove that we "didn't mean anything" by our actions, we would all be better off. We waste a lot of time and energy walking on eggshells after the fact instead of addressing issues openly and determining in that moment the best way to proceed. Imagine the effect this waste of time and energy has on productivity.

Say, I didn't mean anything by it when I said "I want to dance on your grave." I was just caught up in the moment.

One Word Is All It Takes

You're standing in line to board an aircraft. You're eagerly anticipating the delightful food, ample leg room, and five-year-old copies of *Canadian Bow Hunter Monthly* awaiting you on board when the person behind you mentions that the in-flight movie is "Howard the Duck." You exclaim, "Great! We're stuck on a plane with that BOMB!"

Before you can blink, you're being detained, questioned, and treated to a quaint full-body cavity search.

Sometimes one ill-chosen word in the wrong situation is all it takes to create havoc. Yet the power of words and the manner in which they're spoken is still often underestimated.

How we respond to certain words and phrases depends on a number of factors:

- *Location* — Where and when it's being said. Yell, "Fire!" at the top of your lungs in the middle of a Kansas wheat field. Then yell, "Fire!" at a quiet moment during a play in a crowded Broadway theater. Compare your results.

- *Source* — Who's saying it. Women who are strongly committed to feminism in the business world may refer to their socializing together as a "girls' night out." However, this is not recommended phrasing by men.

- *Familiarity* — A close relationship with the source. The same joke enjoyed by three close friends at a backyard party might offend them if they heard it told by a stranger speaking from the podium at a business luncheon.

- *Context* — How it's being used. Using the word "murder" to describe how HugeCo Industries is treating the environment is more benign than using it to describe how one human being is treating another.

Knowing the Right Words

It's not possible for one person to know all the right words to say, especially in a culture where the "correct" or "acceptable" phrase seems to change monthly. Certain people do have preferences. To assume that we know those preferences is to invite misunderstanding and conflict.

One way to avoid choosing the wrong words is to take responsibility for educating ourselves by observing, reading, and adapting to interactions. Another way to avoid choosing the wrong words is simply to ask people about their preferences. Likewise, when you're offended by something said to you, *speak up!* You can turn the situation into an opportunity to enlighten the other person about your preferences. Yet be careful how you do it!

For example, you are in a conversation in which negative stereotypical comments are made about the deaf community. You have a deaf family member. You can choose your response; remember, between every stimulus and response ... there is a choice.

- *Don't act wounded.* Acting wounded may cause you to sit, pout, and withdraw. The purpose is to right a wrong, not demonstrate your level of sensitivity and anger.

- *Don't preach.* Many times no offense was meant, and the person was simply clueless. Getting on your soapbox to "enlighten" the other person may create barriers to communication rather than educate.

- *Be positive.* Capitalize on the chance to make known what is acceptable to you. Tell a story about your family member which helps to educate in a non-threatening manner. You can offer insight in a positive way because of your experience.

Maintaining Energy and Productivity

Think back to the last time you were offended by another person — the co-worker who refused to see things your way, the supervisor who insisted you see things his/her way, the spouse who wasn't listening when you were talking about the offense with that co-worker who wouldn't see things your way or supervisor who ... you get the idea.

Think of how much time and energy you spent on being offended. Now double it. The impact of the offense and conflict goes far beyond the face-to-face interactions, so you spent more energy and time than you thought.

It's human nature to brood over our offenses, conflicts, disagreements, and misunderstandings. Most are followed by familiar thoughts that begin like these ...

"What I SHOULD have said was ...

"Next time I see that person, I'll ...

"I bet my supervisor told everybody. Well, I'll tell them MY side of the story ..."

In short, we're in danger of being consumed by an offense, regardless of its size. *Offense, conflict, and the thoughts that follow take valuable time.* Needless to say, a person in the throes of an unnecessary or extended conflict is not very productive.

When all is said and done, it's the relationship that counts. Poor relationships, or lack of any relationship, lead to lower productivity. Learning to stay off the eggshells can lead to an environment in which employees are free to direct their energy and productivity to more positive ends. That energy can be directed toward developing healthy relationships with co-workers. Innovation and productivity also can occur in relationships in which there are healthy differences of opinion — healthy communication and conflict.

The Platinum Rule

Sometimes we become wakefully challenged (a.k.a. tired) of being politically correct all the time. It's hard. It takes energy. It's easier to avoid the whole issue and treat everyone the same way.

Yeah, right. This well-intentioned trap we all fall into is the Golden Rule:

*"Do unto **others** as **you** would have **them** do unto you."*

This premise assumes that another person is just like you. That's not always true.

Be honest with yourself:

- Do you treat your parents the same way you treat your siblings?
- Do you treat each of your children in exactly the same way?
- Do you treat all of your friends the same way?

For most of us, the answer is "no."

If you left it up to others to decide how they wanted to be treated, they'd prefer the Platinum Rule:

> "Do unto me as **I want** done unto me. (And leave **your** preferences out of it!)"

You may prefer public recognition — to be in the limelight — while a co-worker may want a simple, private thank you or a formal letter in a personnel file. Treat people as individuals and, therefore, differently based on their uniqueness. We simply need to expand that understanding and adapt it to the workplace. In other words, treat others as they would like to be treated.

Pull Your Head Out of the Sand by Using Positive Confrontation

What should you do when you find yourself walking on eggshells? Following is a chapter summary and a few suggestions of how you can take immediate action.

1 *Acknowledge that the conflict, disagreement, or misunderstanding exists.* Ignoring the conflict will not make it disappear. It's just more difficult to address. "It seems like we are approaching this from different perspectives. Let's talk about that first."

2 *Assess and clarify what the conflict is.* What are the issues? What are you specifically trying to resolve/address? In other words, what's really bugging you?

3 *Be willing to explore the workstyles and methods of other people.* Remember that we all have our own ways of dealing with uncomfortable situations. State what you observe and how it differs from your method, like, "I tend to make decisions quickly based on just the facts. Are you comfortable with that or do we need to have a more in-depth discussion?"

4 *Move beyond fear to a deeper, more realistic understanding of other people.* Educate yourself about them. How? It may be as simple as:

   • Going to another part of town (or somewhere you haven't been before) and eating ethnic foods you've never tried before. Observe the people around you.

   • Looking in the community events section of your local newspaper every few months. Choose one event outside of your comfort zone to attend … and attend!

   • Going to a community function where you are in the minority.

- Doing something that is uncomfortable or out of character for you: go to a movie alone, eat out in a nice restaurant alone, etc., to help you feel the emotions of being different or isolated.

This is a short list of suggestions to help you begin to develop a deeper, more realistic understanding of people who are different from you.

5   *Keep a check on your emotions.* Become aware of your own anger and frustrations. Admitting to yourself when you're angry, uncomfortable, or confused is half the battle. That's how we avoid letting emotions build to an explosive state or seep out sideways hurting people with whom we have no disagreement. Once we are aware of the negative emotion, we can choose to redirect it to promote inclusion.

6   *Take a stand.* Be willing to speak out against intolerance. And don't be afraid to gently let other people know about your preferences. Remember to say it in a way so that they *want* to listen and *want* to adapt. Instead of saying, "I can't attend the meeting," try saying something like, "That day is our most sacred religious day, and I need to spend it with my family. Could we consider changing the date so I could attend?"

7   *Let the person know what you want and need.* You will usually be disappointed when you expect others to be mind readers. For instance, you might say, "Since we're running short on time, I think we need to stay focused on our original goal."

8   *Ask for feedback on others' wants and needs and incorporate them into the solution.* Asking others what they need is a powerful way to draw them in, and include them in the team. Just asking for feedback isn't good enough. Nothing is worse than being asked for input, then having it discarded or ignored.

9   *Confront difficult situations.* Be courageous! Ask the difficult questions to avoid future conflicts. Call the behavior. If Tom seems frustrated, say, "Tom, you seem frustrated. Why?" It can be that simple.

10 *Get a commitment from all involved to work toward a successful resolution.* Without unanimous agreement, conflict and misunderstandings cannot be properly managed. Everyone must make a firm commitment, either verbal or written.

11 *Be clear on your intent and agree on an end result.* By stating your intention and sharing the impact or end result openly, you and others know where you're headed. Create space for others to share their intentions and impact too. Assume others have good intent. It will help us all move forward faster. Yet, life isn't always perfect, so be willing to compromise while being honest about what you want.

12 *Don't assume, ask! Resist the impulse to assume you know something about another based on a stereotype.* It's not the responsibility of any minority to educate the masses about an entire group of people. Try, "How did you learn to cook so well?" instead of, "You people all cook so well. Why is that?"

13 *Make a case for how you can win by positively confronting situations and not avoiding them.* Work together so that everyone wins. How?

Confront issues, not people.

Consider how others address issues. Learn from their positive examples.

Don't avoid a difficult situation. That's the same as actively trying to create a new one. Both are lose/lose situations.

Join a group whose membership gives you the opportunity to connect with people different from yourself.

Remember — you have the power to influence the situations in which you find yourself.

14 *Write down two ways others might walk on eggshells with you* (your hot buttons or triggers).

   1.

   2.

15 *Write down two ways you can avoid walking on eggshells or positively deal with a conflict situation at work right now.*

   1.

   2.

Chapter 3

I'm Okay But "They" Need Help: Why should I change?

> *"Things do not change; we do."*
>
> Henry David Thoreau
> *U.S. American essayist, naturalist, poet*

Russian author, Leo Tolstoy (*War and Peace*), once commented that everyone wants to change the world but few want to change themselves. Yet, improving any situation can only begin when the most important initial change of all occurs — a personal change of mind and heart.

I'd like to propose that we adopt a dress code and guidelines for hygiene because those people really need it.

Such is the case when dealing with issues of diversity. But making a personal change in how we deal with people different from us may not be at the top of everybody's "To Do" list. In fact, you may have heard (or even felt) these sentiments:

"Why do we spend so much time flapping our lips about diversity instead of concentrating on 'just getting the job done'?

"We're sick of hearing about and getting beat up over this diversity stuff!

"This has nothing to do with business. It's just more touchy-feely nonsense thrown into an otherwise professional workday."

Again I Ask, "Why Should I Change?"

Because change will make conducting business easier. With every change we experience, we have the opportunity to develop more flexibility, adaptability, and resilience.

What would you do if someone took away your phone? Your computer? Your fax machine? Voice mail? Internet access? It would be tough to survive in today's business world without them. That's why U.S. businesses spend $1 trillion annually on new technology (National Public Radio, January 15, 1998).

Technological advances are such an indispensable part of everyday work that it's hard to imagine that each one met some form of resistance when it was introduced. *Just as you keep up with technological advances in the workplace, you must also keep up with the changing workforce.* That means dealing with human diversity issues.

But What If I Just Don't Care?

Okay, if you're going to be a stickler about it, let's get a dose of reality ...

Check out these statistics for the U.S.:

- Currently the Hispanic population is more than 30 million and is projected to grow to 41 million by 2010. The Hispanic population is growing at an annual rate of 3.5% as compared to whites at 0.5%.[1]

- The Asian American population is 10.2 million, with an average age of 30.1 years, the highest average household income and the highest level of education as compared to all other consumers.[2]

- By the year 2020, the African American population is expected to reach 45 million.[2]

- One in every four U.S. Americans is from a minority population, according to the 2000 Census.

- The population of the U.S. was 264 million in 1995 and is estimated to be 394 million in 2050. According to the Minority Business Development Agency, U.S. Department of Commerce, the minority population will account for nearly 90 percent of the total growth of 131 million people.

So what?

If the U.S. is changing so dramatically then the labor force in the U.S. will continue to diversify.

The Workplace Is Changing!

Think your current workplace isn't diverse? Wait a year. Or a week. Or a day. The people you work with in the future could be vastly different from the people you've worked with in the past or are working with today. We all need to adapt to get the most from all the people around us.

"There is a fear of what lies ahead, but I've found from experience that this fear changes to strength."

Mary Robinson
United Nations High
Commissioner
Former President of Ireland

The snapshot of today's workforce reveals diverse work teams that predictions say will become even more diverse as the demographics change. In studies conducted as far back as 1977, research found that diverse work teams are more productive in the long-term, are more innovative and creative, and are better at problem-solving and decision-making. However, initially there will be greater conflict, more attrition, and less cohesion. We need to be prepared for the initial bumps in the road knowing that, in the long term, the outcomes of diverse work groups are significantly better.[3]

Don't believe it? Consider these facts:

- Workforce demographics have dramatically shifted in the last two decades.

- Women account for 60 percent of the U.S. workforce.[4]

- According to the National Federation for Women Business Owners, women-owned firms represent 30 percent of all businesses, employing 27.5 million people and generating more than $3.6 trillion a year. That's more than the GNP of most countries.

- The percentage of U.S. women participating in the workforce has been climbing steadily since 1970. In 1970, less than 60 percent of women aged 25-54 were in the workforce. Projections for 2005 jump to 80-90 percent.[5]

- The percentage of U.S. men participating in the labor force has been declining. In 1948, more than 85 percent of men were employed. That figure fell to little more than 70 percent in 1995.[5]

- Immigrants make up a large part of our workforce growth. In 1980, immigrants were only 6.4 percent of the U.S. workforce, but were responsible for about one quarter of workforce growth in the 1980s. In 1994, immigrants made up 9.4 percent of the U.S. workforce, yet were responsible for about half of the workforce growth in the 1990s. The change in immigration policies can greatly impact the make-up of the U.S. workforce in the future, as it has in the past.[4]

- The workforce across the U.S. reflects the make-up of specific regions, and demographic growth varies greatly depending on where you are in the U.S. For example, by 2020, the U.S. Census Bureau says California will be 42 percent Hispanic, 18 percent Asian, with less than one-third being white. The workforce in California will reflect that population.

- According to the U.S. Census 2000, the average age in the workforce is in the mid-30's.

- Census projections also indicate that, by the year 2030, the population over age 65 will reach 70.3 million, compared with 34.8 million in the year 2000. Aging baby boomers (those born between 1945 – 1965) will dramatically affect the U.S. workplace because they will live longer, work past traditional retirement age, require new and different services, and shift public policy.

So what?

The workforce is growing slowly, becoming more female, older and includes more minorities; people who learn to communicate effectively in a diverse environment will have an advantage over those who don't.

Customers Are Changing!

Money is being spent differently than it has been in the past.

- Women are credited with making 80% of purchase decisions and account for more than 50% of the spending in the United States.[6]

- Gays and lesbians have the purchasing power of $450 billion dollars annually.[7]

- According to the Minority Business Development Agency, minority purchasing power could be as high as $4.3 trillion by 2045.

- Spending has changed dramatically in the United States over the years. Advertising is becoming more culturally sensitive. The internet-driven world has presented marketers with unprecedented opportunities. After taking a look at the chart below regarding buying power, no one would question why a company markets their products to targeted groups.

($ in Billions)		
1990	**2001** (projected)	**% change in buying power**
Native Amer.	$19.2	$34.8	+81.0
Asian	$112.9	$253.4	+124.8
Hispanic	$207.5	$452.4	+118.0
African Amer.	$307.7	$572.0	+85.9
Whites	$3,715.0	$6,219.8	+70.4

Source: Selig Center for Economic Growth, University of GA, 2000

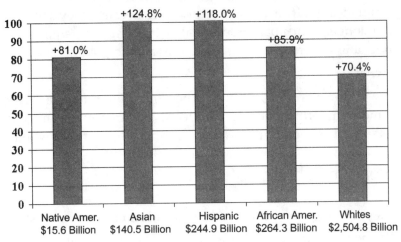

Increase of Purchasing Power from 1990-2001

Native Amer.	Asian	Hispanic	African Amer.	Whites
+81.0%	+124.8%	+118.0%	+85.9%	+70.4%
$15.6 Billion	$140.5 Billion	$244.9 Billion	$264.3 Billion	$2,504.8 Billion

So what?

Businesses that understand the nuances of marketing to an ever-evolving customer base will benefit with new opportunities to expand market reach and attract new business.

The Marketplace Is Changing!

Specifically, the marketplace is becoming more global.

According to the book *Workforce 2020: Work and Workers in the 21st Century*, ongoing and fluctuating changes in the workplace and customer base will continue to shift the U.S. economy by:

- *Expanding the markets for products and services* — everything from shampoo to financial services

- *Increasing competition* — companies must change or die

- *Decreasing monopolies* — AT&T no longer monopolizes U.S. American telephony

- *Continuing the shift from industrial/goods to information/ services* — at the dawn of the twentieth century, 63 percent of U.S. workers produced goods and 37 percent produced services. The Bureau of Economic Analysis estimates that by the year 2025, 83 percent of the U.S. workforce will be in the service sector.

Not understanding the language and cultural nuances of people different from us can lead to some hilarious but costly mistakes. You may have heard the stories:

- When Pepsi came up with the slogan, "Come Alive with the Pepsi Generation" in the 1960s, it had no idea it was dabbling in the occult. The Mandarin translation for the slogan was, "Pepsi will bring your ancestors back from the dead!"

> "If companies are to compete in the changing marketplace, and if they are to treat all employees with equal respect, diversity is essential."
> "White, Male, and Worried"
> Business Week
> January 31, 1994

- A Parker pen appeared in ads in Mexico with the line, "It won't leak in your pocket and embarrass you." Sounds like a solid, safe endorsement. But a bad choice of verbs (copywriters thought "embarazar" meant "embarrass") gave the pen powers its creators never knew it had: "It won't leak in your pocket and make you pregnant."

- Another Spanish translation added some unwanted spice to Frank Purdue's chicken. "It Takes a Tough Man to Make a Tender Chicken" became "It Takes a Virile Man to Make a Chicken Aroused."

Need any other reasons to achieve a greater understanding of business on a global scale?

- In only 6 months, spending on mergers and acquisitions across international borders rose 60% to an all-time, high of $643 billion with a new benchmark of 3,310 announced deals.[8]

- During the year 2000 alone, United States imports totaled more than $1.4 billion dollars. That equates to $370 million more imports than exports.[8] According to the United States Census statistics, imports and exports are growing rapidly. In the last 40 years they have more than quadrupled with expectations that the trend will continue.

- From 1990 to 1999 global trade rose 60% to $5.5 trillion.[9] With the marketplace changing so rapidly we can expect global trade to rise even more in the first decade of the 21st Century.

- Market capitalization has increased almost five-fold during the past ten years in developing countries, from $485 billion in 1990 to $2,243 billion in 2000.[9]

So what?

The rest of the world impacts the U.S. economy to a degree that it never did in the past as evidenced by the fast growing Asian and Latin American markets that present both challenges and opportunities. U.S. manufacturing is now integrated into global markets. Many U.S. manufacturing jobs are dependent more and more on export markets. With advanced communications technologies, such as the use of the internet for real-time information exchange and file transfer, distance is no longer an obstacle for global relations.

Our Approach to Work Is Changing!

Gone are the days of the cradle-to-grave job. And gone are the days when parents wouldn't hesitate to miss a school program or child's baseball game because "duty calls."

Today's worker is less willing to assimilate and conform to rigid corporate work rules, whether written ("Workers are expected to be present during regular business hours of 8 a.m. to 5 p.m.") or unwritten ("If there's extra work to be done, you work nights and weekends."). Because workers' priorities are changing, many businesses are changing to accommodate those priorities. These changes include:

- *Flexible work schedules* — Varied family structures and greater emphasis on work/life balance call for less rigidly structured work hours.
- *Dress code* — Whether it's "casual Friday" or all week long, some businesses have acknowledged that some employees are more comfortable and do better work when they "dress down." Other businesses are revisiting the value of business rather than casual attire.
- *Changing benefits* — More and more companies are extending domestic benefits to non-traditional families.

- *Subsidized or onsite child care* — companies are finding that parents are more secure when their children are close by or in onsite day care facilities.

- *Family leave and family care policies* — companies are responding not only to federal guidelines, but to the needs of workers who give primary care to aging parents or critically ill family members.

So what?

Companies are recognizing the value of caring for their greatest asset — human capital! Rewards for the highly educated workers who can create and apply new technologies will increase significantly by the year 2020. At the same time, the U.S. workforce could be the most flexible, prosperous and intellectually stimulated that we have ever known. We can only achieve this goal if we understand others, positively confront our challenges, and take personal responsibility for acquiring that understanding to a new level.

It's the Law — and It Can Cost You!

Ever hear of Affirmative Action? How about freedom from religious persecution? Sexual harassment, perhaps? Equal access laws to benefit the disabled? Or what about age discrimination? If you don't understand these anti-discrimination laws, learn about them now. It'll save valuable time that you won't be able to spare while you're in the middle of a multi-million dollar lawsuit.

Even with widespread publicity about the perils of discrimination, it appears that many U.S. businesses have not yet addressed the problem. This is a clear and present danger to companies that face an increasing liability risk. As far back as 1988, a typical Fortune 500 corporation could expect to lose $6.7 million annually from absenteeism, low productivity, increased health care costs, low morale, and employee turnover. This does not include the actual cost of a suit or damage to the company's image.[10] More recently the government reported a 300% increase in discrimination lawsuits: up from 7,000 in 1990 to over 21,500 in 1998.[11]

Discrimination lawsuits will cost you. Take a look at how costly discrimination settlements have been for these well-known companies[12]:

- Denny's customer discrimination settlement: $54.4 million
- Home Depot's gender bias settlement: $87.5 million
- Texaco's employee discrimination settlement: $140 million
- Coca-Cola's racial discrimination lawsuit: $156 million
- Ford Motor Co. paid $10.5 million to settle two class-action lawsuits accusing it of discriminating against older white men in the name of diversity
- Charges have been filed in a $5 billion lawsuit against Microsoft for racial discrimination against African American employees and discrimination against female employees.

So, think again about the importance and impact of "this diversity stuff." Start by dwelling on the advantages, rather than the things that may tick you off.

You Snooze! You Lose!

If you refuse to adapt to the changing workforce, you risk isolating yourself from those around you and from the business itself. That can mean less pay, fewer promotions, and lack of respect. It can also have a serious negative impact on your corporation's bottom line.

> "What is the difference between an obstacle and an opportunity? Our attitude toward it. Every opportunity has a difficulty, and every difficulty has an opportunity."
>
> J. Sidlow Baxter
> Pastor, author

Before you are willing to change, the motivation/benefits must be made clear. Always ask the question, "How do I benefit from adapting?" and search for the WIIFM ("what's in it for me?"). When you embrace diversity, the people around you and the company aren't the only ones who benefit. You benefit as well.

Advantages of Embracing Diversity

You become more:

- Global in your perspective

- Knowledgeable about your world
- Comfortable in a wide variety of settings
- Marketable in a newly global environment
- Valued as an intelligent, fair-minded and responsible person.

   With these advantages at your fingertips, who wouldn't want to explore the rewards of embracing diversity?

Elements of Change

When Changes Begin

   Let's look at common concerns you and your fellow employees may have in response to changes and transitions in the work environment. (As you read, make note of key words that describe feelings you've had in the past or are experiencing now.)

   Feelings — In times of transition and change in the work environment, many employees experience intense feelings of:

- Loss
- Grief
- Depression
- Inadequacy
- Insecurity
- Anger.

This intensity may be compounded if it appears to go unnoticed by managers, co-workers, and even family members. These feelings may lead to questions of personal and professional competency or of the employees' value to the organization.

Adjusting — Employees may have a tough time adjusting emotionally, psychologically, and stylistically to a new organization environment and new policies. Their styles, skills, philosophies, and approaches may be out of sync with changing directions and focuses within the company.

New Tasks, New Roles — New job descriptions may involve tasks, technologies, and skills that employees do not feel they possess. They may wonder how much time they have to adjust to new roles and may be anxious about successfully adapting their abilities to these changes.

Long-term Effects — Many people remain worried long after organizational change has occurred. They are concerned about future possibilities for promotion and advancement — and wonder about their future options and opportunities to grow and develop.

With these concerns popping up in the wake of change, it's no wonder people hesitate to dive into it. The difference is in the approach we take toward confronting these concerns. You can choose to see it as an obstacle or an opportunity.

Before We Start the Big Stuff ...

Here are some important things to keep in mind about the nature of change:

- *Anyone can be a role model for change* — One person can be the stimulus for change, regardless of how few people come into contact with that individual. Sometimes we learn from unlikely places ... hence the phrase, "Out of the mouths of babes." Or how about public policy changes resulting from one woman named Rosa Parks in Alabama who refused to move the back of the bus?

- *Change usually involves risk* — Sweeping changes begin with one person willing to take a risk. Up until the mid-19th Century, many people thought that eating tomatoes caused sexual hysteria. Imagine being the first person who put his/her reputation on the line by eating a tomato in public without succumbing to a lustful rampage. When that person's behavior didn't change, imagine how relieved everyone felt. Or how disappointed!

- *One has to be willing and able* — Willingness and ability are quite different. Sometimes people say they *can't* change

when they really mean they don't know *how* to or don't
want to. People need to have the necessary knowledge,
skills, and confidence to change.

- *Actions speak volumes* — No
matter where you are in a
company or in your
community, somebody's
watching you and
learning from you. If
others see the choices
we make and the
consequences or
rewards as a result
of those choices, we
have the chance to
make a real difference.

Okay. Let's say you're
convinced that change has its rewards. You are officially fired up about
making a change or two to benefit the greater good (remember, you
could be the next risk-taking tomato-eater to win praise and admiration
from your coworkers and family!).

"How do I start?"

Glad you asked!

What You Know and Don't Know

When it comes to diversity, we often don't know what we don't
know. In every interaction we have with others, there is an element of
the unknown. We know things that
others don't and others know things
that we don't that help us create our
perceptions in life.

> *"You can't change what you
> won't acknowledge."*
>
> Dr. Phil McGraw
> *Psychologist, author*

This concept was put into an easy-
to-understand model (on next page)
called the Johari Window, named after its creators, Joseph Luft and
Harry Ingham.[13]

Johari Window: Four combinations of knowledge

	What others know	What others don't know
What I know	**PUBLIC** What we all know	**PRIVATE** What I know and others don't know
What I don't know	**BLIND SPOTS** What others know and I don't know	**UNKNOWN** What no one knows ... yet

Explanation

"Public" Knowledge. This level of knowledge includes an awareness of characteristics, actions, feelings, and wants by all parties. These are messages we intentionally convey to, or share with, others that make up our public personalities. Typically this is where we are most comfortable.

"Private" Knowledge. This refers to being aware of your characteristics, actions, feelings, and wants but others are not aware of them. This is your private persona that might include something as simple as your passion for chocolate-dipped potato chips. Or it can be more complex, such as expert knowledge that could be used to teach and educate others.

"Blind Spots" Knowledge. This refers to not being aware of your characteristics, actions, feelings, and wants but others are aware of them. These are your "blind spots." Your blind spots might be the very thing you most need to see. Exploring your blind spots gives you an opportunity for growth and learning by asking for feedback and observing other people.

"Unknown" Knowledge. This level of knowledge is one in which all parties are unaware of their characteristics, actions, feelings, and wants, even though this unknown knowledge may affect the relationship. We like to have the answers. Unfortunately, when we are here, we don't even know the questions!

"Public" knowledge offers us comfort and familiarity. Yet, comfort doesn't afford much opportunity for growth. By striving to pry open the blind spots and unknown windows of our knowledge, we invite positive personal change into our lives through heightened awareness.

Self-Awareness and Understanding

Personal change begins when we ask ourselves some tough questions:

- What assumptions and generalizations drive our behaviors? (Are we aware of why we feel the way we do?)

- Where does the information that we have about others come from? (Past experience? Parents? Geography? Hearsay? Television? Movies? News stories?)

- How reliable is that information? (Are we putting more trust in Homer Simpson or Jay Leno than our personal experience?)

Understanding and empathy follow increased knowledge — *the more we know about others, the less we fear them.*

Perhaps the toughest question we have to ask ourselves is:

What kind of impact does our own behavior have on others?

To answer these questions, we can incorporate a method of self-examination that's simple, thorough, painless — and caffeine-free!

Head, Heart, and Hand

True self-awareness around diversity issues comes when we employ the *"Head, Heart, and Hand"* method to examine how we feel about a person, a thing, an idea, etc. Interculturalists as far back as 1904 have called this the "cognitive, affective, behavioral" model. Other practitioners call it the "think, feel, do" model.

Head — What do we **know** and what do we **think**?

Heart — How do we **feel** about it? What do I **want**?

Hand — How will we **act** — based on what we think and how we feel together?

To see how it works, let's use the Head, Heart, and Hand method to examine our feelings about something non-controversial — pizza.

> *Head* — I **know** pizza is made up of crust, sauce, cheese, meat, and vegetables. I **think** certain combinations of these ingredients could taste very good.
>
> *Heart* — MMM…I **love** pizza — Pizza rules! **Want**: *I want a pizza and I want it now!*
>
> *Hand* — **Call** the delivery guy! Gee, do I have to do *everything* around here?

Now let's apply the Head, Heart, and Hand model to a meeting scenario and see how the outcome (hand) is directly impacted by the thoughts (head) and feelings (heart):

> *Head* — I **know** Andre has interrupted me in a department meeting. This is the third time he has interrupted me in front of other people. *I may **think**: 1) he doesn't think I have anything of value to add, 2) he thinks his ideas are more important than mine, 3) he was excited with my idea and wanted to offer his own.*
>
> *Heart* — I am **angry** with Andre. **Want**: *He must stop interrupting me.*
>
> *Hand* — **Interrupt** him back, speak louder, and more forcefully until he understands what I want.

This is a typical automatic response. It's obvious that the perceived negative behavior from Andre created negative thoughts and emotions that caused me to react negatively. One bad turn deserves another– right?

Wrong.

Taking time to assess the information that comes from answering self-awareness questions and applying the Head, Heart, and Hand model will help us in determining what skills and competencies we may need in order to modify or change our behaviors.

Let's use the Head, Heart, and Hand model to change our reaction in this same situation.

> *Head* — I **know** Andre has interrupted me in a department meeting. This is the third time he has interrupted me in front of other people. *I may **think**: 1) he*

doesn't think I have anything of value to add, 2) he thinks his ideas are more important than mine, 3) he was excited with my idea and wanted to offer his own. **Ask myself**: I wonder if he's aware that he's interrupting me?

Heart — <u>My interpretation</u> of the fact that Andre has interrupted me is that he doesn't think I have anything of value to add so I am **angry** with Andre. It upsets and even hurts me to be interrupted. *Want: He must stop interrupting me. I want Andre and me to communicate more effectively with each other.*

Hand — **Talk** to Andre privately and ask if he is aware that he has been interrupting me. **Explain** the impact of his behavior on me and my behavior. **Work** with him to reach a joint commitment to improve our communication with each other.

Modeling

The more self-aware we are the more likely we are to model appropriate behavior. *It's impossible to change behavior of which we are not aware.*

Remember the last person you stood next to who was drenched in too much cologne — and really stunk? I mean full-blown, eye-watering, deodorant-denying, wallpaper-peeling gagacious? Try for a moment to remember just how bad the smell was. (Don't try too hard. Remember — we just ordered pizza.)

Now, did that person realize how offensive s/he really was? Chances are, no.

Most of us don't. We go through our workday mostly unconscious of our behavior toward others. We have little awareness of how our actions impact and affect others. We may be oblivious to the fact that we're **modeling**—*providing an example of behavior patterns for others to follow.* No matter how hard we try to convince ourselves and others that our influence is minimal, *our own beliefs and conduct can affect the attitudes and behaviors of others.*

People may even follow your behavior when you don't want them to do so! Neither children nor adults respond well to the old adage, "Do as I say, not as I do."

At what point did we get to "do as I *say*, not as I *do*?" To what do we owe our attitudes about what people think of us? It could be:

Lack of awareness — Not paying attention to what we're doing and how others observe us.

Naiveté — An uninformed assumption that "nobody's watching."

Work pressures — A heavy load and full schedule leave little time to notice others noticing us.

Ethnocentrism — We can also call this egocentrism, which is the belief that we're the center of the universe. (We'll go into more detail on this in Chapter 5.)

Confrontation

How can we tell if we're modeling inappropriate behavior?

- Co-worker(s) become quiet and withdrawn.
- Co-worker(s) become angry and/or confrontational or passive/aggressive.
- Boss or supervisor requests a "meeting" regarding behavior. (This one's pretty hard to miss.)
- We're fired. (Just try to ignore THAT one.)

The reality is, *if we don't deal with our sometimes inappropriate behaviors, they can come back to haunt us.*

So, how do we respond to co-workers who confront us about our behavior? There are several options:

Bad Responses to Confrontation

Ignoring the person or comment — This will cause further resentment and will require the person to bring in a supervisor or boss to mediate what could have been settled without third-party intervention.

More of the same behavior — Meeting aggression with aggression will only fuel the fire and prove their point. We could call this insanity — doing the same thing over and over and expecting different results.

Fisticuffs — This may enter our minds but it's totally inappropriate. Throwing a punch at someone who takes a risk to talk with you about the impact of your behavior will only lead to bigger problems. Find a resolution together by openly discussing options and coming to a mutual understanding or compromise.

Good Responses to Confrontation

Suspend judgment — The confrontor may have a point or may just be misinformed. Be sure to gather all the facts and refrain from jumping to your own conclusion.

Listen — Pay attention to what is truly being said as though hearing from an expert. What is the true meaning?

Evaluate objectively — Determine whether or not the person has a valid concern. Ask yourself: How can the team, the goal, or you personally be negatively impacted? Could this person actually have a good point?

Empathize — Put yourself in other people's shoes to experience the same feelings they have. See the situation — and yourself — from their perspective.

A confrontation is a good sign that a change needs to be made, either on the part of one or both of the parties involved. Part of that change is modifying behavior.

Modifying Behavior (and why it's so hard to do)

Like any change, modifying behavior requires a lot from us. Most notably, it may require us to do things differently than we have for years ... or for our entire lives.

How do we start changing patterns of behavior that seem as permanent as granite, sturdy as redwoods, yet as outdated as a leisure suit? A good place to start is to examine how we communicate.

Stop Talking — Start a Dialogue

Any good confrontation begins and ends with clear, well-understood communication.

Or does it?

According to Webster's Dictionary, to *communicate* means, "to give or pass on information." On the other hand, Webster says a *dialogue* is a "conversation between two or more people." So, according to these definitions, information is actually "exchanged" during a dialogue.

Too often we are in a hurry to communicate information, especially information with which we are uncomfortable. We rush through it, saying the words at record speed with only one objective in mind: to get to the last word of the last sentence of the last paragraph.

Confrontation, anyone? Given the above definitions of "communication" and "dialogue," you may jump at the chance to initiate "good" confrontation by seeing it as having an open dialogue.

Many times when we communicate we hope a dialogue, not a debate, will ensue. Dialogue sets the stage for trust and is an open forum to share perspectives, not necessarily to reach conclusions. If trust is to be established between all levels of the organization, we must provide more opportunities for dialogue to occur. *Remember, relationships are the key to working through diversity issues.*

How Do I Know If It's Really a Dialogue?

True dialogue has a number of characteristics. True dialogue:
- Seeks underlying meaning
- Allows those involved to see both sides
- Results in new understanding
- Strengthens both parties rather than exploiting either one
- Benefits both parties by producing a win/win result.

Guidelines of True Dialogue

The principles of dialogue must be adhered to if the above results are to be achieved:

Suspension — Explore your own thinking about that person: "She's too aggressive," "He's a racist," etc. Temporarily suspend your judgment, feelings, and/or attitudes about the person with whom you're having a conflict.

Identify the source of assumptions — Ask yourself where those assumptions are coming from. "What messages did I get (and continue to hold on to) about this person or group of people?"

Listen for meaning — Listen with a willingness to be influenced. But don't ignore your "self-talk," which will alert you if you begin to compromise what you hope to attain. Achieving true dialogue doesn't mean you have to agree with every point that's presented.

Balance inquiry and advocacy — Ask questions from a place of not knowing. For instance, "Can you help me understand your thinking?" Dig deeper. Get information. Then share your information with others in an attempt to help that person understand you better.

Reflection — Allow time to reflect and focus on what is going on in the present.

And by the Way ... Play Nicely!

Everyone has a right to be treated with respect as an individual without being blind-sided by information. That's especially true in a healthy dialogue. Respect others enough to allow expression of their thoughts and feelings without being subjected to embarrassment or fear. Here are some signs of courtesy:

- Allow for time in regular meetings and in one-on-one interactions for others to express their thoughts and create action plans.

- Listen! Sometimes all we need is for someone to listen, not fix the issue. Unless it was asked for, the advice is quickly dismissed anyway.

- Recognize that each person has a life outside the organization and, try as they might, cannot always keep home issues from affecting their workday.

Evaluating Communication Styles

We all move from one communication style to another depending on the situation. However, we typically have a style that we use most often because it's the one with which we are usually the most comfortable. How do you communicate information to your employees or co-workers, especially when you are feeling threatened, insecure, nervous, confused, or challenged? And, what effect does the particular style of delivery have on the employee?

Look at the following list, and think about instances when you have modeled these communication styles. Keep in mind that there is no good or bad, right or wrong associated with each of these styles. Certain situations necessitate a certain style type.

"The Connie Chung/Diane Sawyer Interview," Television News Reporters

Characteristics — Facilitates, interviews, and uses responsive techniques. Asks questions clearly and succinctly.

Effect on others — Feelings of respect, being valued. Power struggles and defensiveness are minimized.

Situational application — This style works well when gathering information. It develops a sense of trust, consistency, consideration, and equality. This style opens the door for two-way communication, so, if you don't want feedback, don't use this style.

"The Dr. Sigmund Freud Ego Trip," Creator of Psychoanalysis

Characteristics — Interpretive, all-knowing. Suggests a certain superiority and wisdom to know what the other person is really thinking.

Effect on others — Could be feelings of inferiority, helplessness, and inadequacy; or appreciation for the wisdom and insightful views.

Situational application — This style works when something is fact-based and there is a right answer. However, while we may sometimes believe we know what others are thinking, we cannot always make that assumption. Don't start a conversation by saying, "I suppose you think that ..."

"The Henry Kissinger Big Picture," U.S. 56th Secretary of State

Characteristics — Has a purpose for the meeting but listens to all sides involved before making a final decision.

Effect on others — Feelings of validation, respect, importance.

Situational application — There are already some good feelings going on here. The people involved feel listened to and realize that, even though a decision has probably already been made, negotiations are possible.

"The Perry Mason Cross-examination," Fictional Lawyer

Characteristics — Interrogative with relentless cross-examination.

Effect on others — Can bring guilt, fear, and intimidation or can command respect for his quest for the truth.

Situational application — Asking questions for clarification is very different from asking questions that lead a person and make the individual feel as though you have a hidden agenda. Ask questions that pertain to the issue, be non-judgmental to the response, and provide feedback to the listener to ensure that you have correctly understood the answer.

"The General George S. Patton My Way or the Highway," U.S. Combat General

Characteristics — No feedback allowed. Orders are given with an expectation of compliance without question.

Effect on others — Could be feelings of rejection, insignificance, or hostility; or may instill confidence and trust in their leader and implies the leader's confidence in their abilities to perform.

Situational application — Sometimes a decision just needs to be made and is not open for discussion for safety reasons, the good of the team, etc. It is a decision made for the team, not by the team, but with the full support of team members.

"The Colin L. Powell Handshake," U.S. 64th Secretary of State

Characteristics — Has a defined statement to make. However, the message is delivered so that the fears and concerns of the listener are acknowledged.

Effect on others — Feelings of respect, validation, consideration.

Situational application — Showing genuine concern and making yourself available for assistance while directing the change communicates respect for their feelings and the impact the information will have on them.

"The Janet Reno Hot Seat," First Woman U.S. Attorney General

Characteristics — Often has to make choices between unpopular solutions. Knows that, regardless of the choice, someone will be unhappy.

Effect on others — Could be feelings of skepticism or frustration; or relief and respect that someone else makes the difficult decision.

Situational application — Being in the hot seat is not particularly comfortable for anyone. However, if this is your role, be clear with your purpose and with yourself. Maintain your integrity and be consistent in how your choices are made. Although your final choice may not be popular with everyone, they will respect you for your process.

"The Jerry Seinfeld Stand Up Act," Comedian

Characteristics — Sees the humor in typical human behaviors. Often this humor is cynical and sarcastic.

Effect on others — Could teach us about our own unproductive behaviors or may frustrate us by pointing out those behaviors.

Situational application — Humor and fun are important aspects in the workplace, but be sure the timing and focus of your humor is appropriate. When directed at specific individuals, this style of humor can be disrespectful. Self-deprecating humor — poking fun at yourself, not others — is usually the safest humor to use in the workplace.

"The Oprah Winfrey Standard of Excellence," Talk Show Host, Actress

Characteristics — Authentic. She says whatever is on her mind. Strives for continuous self-awareness and openly shares her personal failures and successes.

Effect on others — Can put people at ease, and make them comfortable and safe. They want to respond back with the same honesty shown to them.

Situational application — Being authentic by telling your personal feelings and stories encourages others to do so. Realize there is great risk in being vulnerable. While we always want to tell the truth, there are different levels of information appropriate to share with people. Carefully choose how much information to share when taking a stance of openness and authenticity.

While all of these people have noted accomplishments, the styles they represent may or may not be appropriate for you depending on what situation you face. We each have control over how we choose to communicate.

Evaluate how your style impacts those around you and choose accordingly.

Choice and Consequence

Just a few seconds after being born, a baby makes its first declaration — it cries. Granted, it's not easy to decipher the exact words but the meaning is clear: "This isn't what I wanted! I was warm! Now I'm cold! What's the deal? And why didn't somebody check with ME first?"

> "We must be the change we wish to see in the world."
>
> *Mahatma Gandhi*
> *Spiritual and Political Leader*

Thus, we all enter the world with an ethnocentric point of view. Ethnocentricity usually boils down to this:

"My way is the only way, and I simply cannot understand why you don't see it!"

How many of us continue to live with that same perspective throughout our adult lives? What power! If we think that way, we don't need to consider the impact of our actions on others. But, in reality, all of our actions touch others in one way or another.

By simply acknowledging that the world doesn't revolve around you, you begin to determine how the choices you make have an impact on those around you. You have the power to influence how your organization works. You have the ability to behave in ways that can help create an organization that is:

- Supportive
- Responsive
- Equitable
- Respectful.

It's all in the choices you make!

Pull Your Head Out of the Sand by Recognizing the Need for Positive (Personal) Change

What should you do to bring about positive change? Following is a chapter summary and a few suggestions of how you can take immediate action.

1   *Commit to developing your awareness of self, diversity and others.* Start with yourself. It is both the right and smart thing to do. It demonstrates a willingness to listen and to adapt, if necessary.

2   *Acknowledge, understand and talk about your feelings.* Start by asking yourself the critical questions, using the Head, Heart, and Hand method.

   Head — What do you **know** and what do you **think**?

   Heart — How do you **feel** about it? What do you **want**?

   Hand — How will you **act** — based on what you think and how you feel together?

   Realizing this creates an atmosphere that fosters your personal growth in times of transition. By confronting tough issues, you are implementing a plan of action that helps you "get out with the old and on with the new." You're already moving in a positive direction.

3   *Learn how your perceptions and assumptions may lead to inappropriate behavior.* To examine your perceptions, play the "First Thoughts" game with a partner.

   Partner #1 reads *each* of these statements *three times in a row* to Partner #2 with Partner #2 finishing the sentence each time with his/her first thought:

   • *Homeless people are …*

   • *Chiropractors are …*

   • *Catholics believe …*

- *Northerners are ...*
- *Working moms are ...*
- *White men are ...*

Now reverse the process with Partner #2 reading *each* of the following statements to Partner #1 with Partner #1 finishing the sentence each time with his/her first thought:

- *People with disabilities want ...*
- *Southerners are ...*
- *Latins are great ...*
- *In relation to men, women are more ...*
- *African American women are ...*
- *People who are fat are ...*

Notice how your responses are indicative of how you may censor and tailor your behavior so that you can impact others' opinions of you.

4   *Become conscious of your impact on others and their impact on your style, values, beliefs, etc.* How? Be bold enough to ask. And don't resent it if the truth they tell isn't what you wanted to hear. For example, if you ask, "Well, how'd it go?" And the response is, "OK, but I really wanted to participate more. It felt like the decision was already made, and my involvement didn't really matter." You have to be willing to have a conversation about that and not judge the honest input you received. That is very valuable feedback ... if you use it.

5   *Reframe to the positive.* Reframing takes a negative statement that you hear and puts a positive spin on it. The way that an idea is phrased determines the outcome. Instead of allowing negative statements to bombard the workplace, try reframing them. For example, if someone says, "Oh, that's management — you know management; they are always squeezing us for everything we are worth. I'm tired of it!" Gently respond by reframing the statement to something like, "Yes, it must be difficult for management; with so many

initiatives, they have a lot to oversee. They really need to ensure that each team delivers on its goals, or we'll be behind in our projections." Okay, so this example is a bit extreme. Yet, you can't deny that reframing negative statements is a powerful communication skill.

6   *Challenge yourself to lean into discomfort.* You limit your growth if you continue to live in your own little world. Put yourself in situations that will take you outside your comfort zone. For example:

- Start a conversation with someone you don't understand or with whom you disagree

- Have an open conversation and be willing to see the situation from a different point of view. You don't have to agree with it, but you have to try to understand the different perspective.

7   *Acknowledge your values and beliefs.* At the same time, think about how these beliefs express themselves in your daily behavior. Use this exercise:

- List three values by which you guide your life

- List five beliefs that you hold about the world that influence your choices and behavior.

Now ask yourself …

- How do these values and beliefs make an impact on my daily behavior?

- Is there anything I'd like to change about my behaviors?

8   *Show how you feel differently.* When you hear a negative stereotype, state how you feel differently. If you hear an unfair overgeneralization about a group of people, give an experience or opinion that shows how you feel differently. This brings the statement down to a specific instance to personalize it. For example, if someone is supporting a negative stereotype and says, "Don't put Mariah on the team. She's a single mom, and it will be a nightmare for scheduling." You can respond with a

personal experience that shows how your experience is different. Say something like, "In our last project team, we had two single parents and scheduling was not a problem. We set the schedule together as a team. Their contributions were very valuable. We would not have come to the same outcome without their expertise. Let's consider her contributions."

9   *Practice empathic listening.* Sympathy is feeling sorry for someone else. Empathy is your ability to experience someone else's feelings, good or bad. Empathy is a powerful skill that you can develop by taking time to listen and show that you understand. Empathy will not only reduce conflict, but it will also show that the other person is valued. How can you be more open to other emotions?

- Ask, "How would I feel right now if I were _____?" (Actually feel the other person's nervousness, anger, frustration, excitement, etc.)

- Don't allow yourself to judge whether or not the feeling you sense is good or bad/right or wrong. It is impossible to listen when judging.

- Stay focused on the emotion and do not allow a thought to creep in. Acknowledging emotions will drive us to a deeper meaning of the situation.

10 *Make yourself employable in a changing marketplace.* In today's changing world the new employment contracts emphasize mutual responsibility for professional growth. Employment contracts are built on the understanding of "non-dependent trust." This trust is built on two unwritten clauses:

- Employees take responsibility for their own careers
- Companies give them the tools to do so.

Your own skills will take you through life, securing the future you desire. That puts more responsibility on you for remaining employable. Doing so means taking steps to become a strong contributor:

- Acknowledge your feelings and talk about them with your manager/supervisor
- Maintain an upbeat attitude
- Look for opportunities to make your job more interesting, stimulating, and challenging
- Maintain a healthy level of self-esteem
- Don't let job performance fall off
- Look for things to get involved with and increase your worth to the company
- Come up with a "What would I do next?" plan
- Take stock of your current job situation; if you're not satisfied, ask for help
- Stay visible, stick to your work, and document your accomplishments
- Build new relationships, internally and externally, to support new roles and expectations
- Broaden your network and skills
- Create a strategic partnership with your manager/supervisor
- Be clear about your department's or division's long- and short-term goals
- Be positive and supportive, give compliments, and don't use negative or rude language
- Find someone to mentor and someone to mentor you.

11 *Agree to disagree.* Just because it's your opinion and you've had it forever doesn't mean everyone else agrees with it. You'll find people who disagree with you across the globe and across the street. Be prepared to agree to disagree.

12 *Write down two things you can do differently at work* using the concepts covered in this chapter and put them into action:

    1.

    2.

Chapter 4

Helping Others Matter: Unleash the power of diversity

> *"I do not care to belong to a club*
> *that accepts people like me as members."*
>
> Groucho Marx
> U. S. American comedian, actor

Groucho's quip makes little or no sense. Just as senseless is any **exclusionary policy** — a stated, written, or informal practice of purposely keeping someone "out of the loop" in a group, club, or business environment. And it happens a lot, from the school playground at recess to the boardrooms of the corporate world.

People who have been excluded in the work environment are on the receiving end of behaviors with common threads of mean-spiritedness and injustice:

"I wasn't invited to an important meeting and a lot of crucial decisions were made without me."

"One of my ideas was dismissed. Someone else suggested it 10 minutes later and got all the credit for his 'brilliant and original' solution."

"A bunch of employees got together for drinks after work. When they started talking business, they made several key decisions without me."

Read the Groucho Marx remark again. Just as most people would never adhere to such a sentiment, *most people would never CHOOSE to be left out or "kept in the dark" in the workplace.* It doesn't make sense. So, someone else is doing it to them.

The concepts of marginalization (exclusion) and mattering were applied to how we act and treat each other by author and researcher, Nancy K. Schlossberg, President of National Career Development Association, and Professor Emerita at

Don't bother asking Bob, he's always in the dark.

the University of Maryland. Let's take a closer look at the effects of marginalization and mattering.

Marginalization (or "What It's Like to Be on the Outside Looking In")

Every person has experienced and felt the negative impact of being rejected, left out, or excluded. Because it happens often in the business world, the business world has come up with a fancy, ten dollar word for it — **marginalization.**

When We're Marginalized ...

Have you ever been the last person picked for the team? Or been left at a clubhouse door staring at a "Keep Out" sign? Ever notice the conversation screech to a halt when you enter a room full of people? Congratulations! You know what it's like to be marginalized. Take an "Atta boy!" out of petty cash.

In the business world, marginalization takes on a slightly different face. It occurs when:

- A person is excluded from meetings or important projects

- A person is not consulted on important matters that fall under the realm of his/her job description
- A person's ideas and suggestions are not seriously considered
- A person's good work is trivialized ("Anybody could have done THAT.")
- An undeserving employee takes credit for a marginalized employee's work
- A person is ignored and made to feel invisible.

Do any of these situations sound familiar? Remember how it felt to be treated that way? We've all experienced it at one time or another. When we are excluded, we believe others:

- Don't care about us
- Don't understand us
- Aren't interested in us
- Don't want to learn about us.

People who have found themselves excluded report feeling an overwhelming **loss of**:

- Self-esteem
- Self-worth
- Energy
- The sense of contributing to the goals of the business.

This exclusion process can be personally devastating. The drawbacks are almost too numerous to fathom. On a personal level, it:

- Builds anger and resentment
- Destroys self-esteem
- Prevents personal growth
- Lowers productivity.

Marginalization can also hurt an entire business. To exclude just one employee can:

- Deny an entire team access to good ideas and innovative answers to problems
- Foster ignorance of the needs and wants of whole market segments

- Detract from the value of the service or product being offered
- Harm personal and professional relationships
- Keep others locked in their own narrow standards, prohibiting personal growth
- Destroy trust.

At one end of the spectrum, marginalization looks like interrupting a co-worker in a meeting. At the other end of the spectrum, it looks like discrimination, isolation, and even violence. To the person being targeted, there is little distinction of severity along this escalating scale of offensive behavior.

Our view of diversity directly impacts when and how we marginalize others.

"But I don't marginalize anyone!"

Thank you, Saint Whoever You Are, but chances are you have.

When We Marginalize Others ...

We are all capable of marginalizing others, consciously or unconsciously, when we fall back on stereotypes that can lead to unfair assumptions and generalizations. The distortion that occurs when we stereotype can result in exclusionary behaviors and practices.

The equation:

Stereotypes	+	Distortion of unfair assumptions and generalizations	=	Exclusionary behavior and practices

For instance . . .

"I've heard that people of Tom's race are lazy."	+	"Therefore, Tom must be lazy."	=	"Let's avoid giving Tom responsibility on this project."

The process of marginalizing someone may not be as obvious as the example above, but the results are the same. Imagine the loss you, the team, the company, and Tom suffer when this process is at play. From all these negative impacts, defensive behaviors begin to arise that become counterproductive. In the above case, Tom may respond to being "left out of the loop" with:

- Anger
- Resentment
- Vindictiveness
- Punishment
- Withdrawal

And perhaps worst of all ...

- A marked absence of motivation and productivity.

Naturally, these behaviors (particularly the last one, in this case) are then used to justify the rationale for exclusion to take place — "We were right to exclude Tom."

When Marginalization Causes Unwanted Change ...

Others who are excluded may try hard to fit in by attempting to become more like the "in group" they aspire to. Unfortunately, in doing so, they may hold back those characteristics about themselves that make them unique. The organization misses out on the creativity and innovation that come through their shared perspectives.

As the individual withdraws due to discomfort, the team cannot benefit from the input of all of its members, and the workplace remains static, unchanged. The effects of individuals being 'shut down' due to exclusion are far reaching, much more so than we usually imagine.

In the end, *all marginalizing or excluding actions toward individuals who are perceived as different will have direct and negative impacts on the bottom line and personal relationships for all concerned.*

Mattering (or "At Last, We Get to Hear Something Positive in This Chapter")

Contrary to marginalizing behavior, when a person is made to matter in a group or situation, positive impacts occur. **Mattering** *occurs when a person is valued and accepted as being unique, with skills and traits that can benefit the business and others as individuals.* People who matter feel that others:

- Depend on them
- Are interested in them
- Are concerned with their fate
- Identify with them
- Care about them
- Appreciate their contributions.

A personal story (because you matter!)

A few years ago I was fortunate to visit a small village in the interior of Venezuela. The booking agency promised a tour guide would greet me when my plane landed. Eager to start my adventure, I hurried off the plane only to discover that there wasn't a single, solitary person in sight. I was alone and upset … and apparently forgotten. In two seconds flat I went from the heights of anticipation to — you guessed it — the depths of marginalization. But the story doesn't end there …

I called the local phone number I had been given, explained my situation, and in no time at all a tour guide arrived. He showed me the sites of the village. We had interesting conversations. He made me feel comfortable in unfamiliar territory. And, not only did he go out of his way to welcome me after such confusion with the company, but he graciously invited me to his home to have dinner with his family. He lived with his mother, sister, and two young children in a three-room house made of concrete blocks and a cement floor. The family was so concerned about the mishap, they insisted on making two special, family soup recipes. The chicken soup cooked on the two-burner electric stove inside the house and the tortuga (turtle) soup was soon steaming in the black cauldron over the fire in the yard.

With nothing more than friendly conversation and unconditional acceptance, this family made me feel appreciated and included. Single handedly, the tour guide transformed a situation of marginalization into one of mattering.

The moral of the story (because every story should have one) is that we all possess the power to transform marginality into mattering.

When people are treated as though they matter, they act and behave in ways that reflect the positive cues and feelings they are receiving. People who matter:

- Become more productive
- Openly share information
- Feel high levels of trust from others
- Are motivated and dedicated
- Respect others' skills and contributions
- Put the goals of the group ahead of their personal needs and wants.

For example, I came into the above situation with a low level of trust. However, by his words and actions, the guide was able to create a high level of trust. I expressed my appreciation to him personally, and openly praised his effort to the employer, and everyone else who asks about my experience.

Mattering has direct and positive impacts on the bottom line and personal relationships for all concerned.

The Bottom Line on Mattering and Marginality

The value of a diverse work group is in the variety of perspectives brought about as a result of different values, beliefs, age, race, gender, creed, etc., found within that group. All the things that make us different create in each of us a unique way of looking at the world and responding to it. This diversity of perspectives adds value to the products and services our organizations and institutions offer their customers and clients.

> "People and their differences make up the foundation of an organization's ability to develop broad perspectives and to approach business problems in new and creative ways."
>
> Barbara Walker
> Author, Human Resource
> Development expert

But the bottom line on mattering and marginalization is *the bottom line.* People who matter are valued and more productive. More productive workers often mean more profit. People who feel marginalized are less productive. Less productive workers mean less profit.

Gimme One Reason to Stay Here

For some the process of continual workplace marginalization becomes unacceptable. They just leave! Situations become so uncomfortable that it's not worth staying for any amount of money or token prestige.

An Employer of Choice (Yes, there IS such a thing!)

Considering how difficult it is to find and retain the brightest and the most talented employees, it is critical for organizations to become an **Employer of Choice** — *organizations that respect, recognize, and reward employees, allowing them to bring all of who they are into the workplace.*

> *"When work is a pleasure, life is a joy! When work is duty, life is slavery."*
>
> Maxim Gorky
> Russian novelist, playwright

Employers of Choice realize:

- Workers must feel that they matter
- Workers must feel respected
- Workers must be recognized and rewarded
- Departing workers cost money.

Underline that last one. Studies conducted by Global Learning Resources in 2000 show that recruitment, training, and learning curve losses related to departing workers may cost a company up to three times the base salary for a mid-level employee. **Any way you calculate it, replacing employees who leave because they feel like they are not respected and valued costs money.** *Therefore, respecting and utilizing all the human resources is a bottom line matter for any organization.*

Respect

Ask employees what keeps them coming back to work every day, and most will say, "respect," or "the feeling of being valued," or "being a contributing member of a team." Those are easy answers but with complex underpinnings.

What are the characteristics of respect in the workplace?

Acknowledgment that people are different. Not recognizing a person's difference can sometimes be offensive. "Oh, I didn't notice you're a person of color because, you see, I am color-blind." Really??! Claiming *not* to notice people's skin pigment can be a great insult and a futile attempt to show an absence of bias.

> "Without feelings of respect, what is there to distinguish men from beasts?"
>
> Confucius
> Chinese philosopher

An understanding of our differences. A statement such as, "Now I know why you don't speak up in meetings," may actually draw out a person who feels a trusting environment is replacing a marginalizing one.

Treating people as they want to be treated. In Chapter 2 of this book, we learned the Platinum Rule to "Do unto others as they want done unto them," not how WE think they want done unto them. This is the root of the flex-time/flexible working hours policy at many organizations. This doesn't mean management caves in to every worker's demand, but it does mean making an effort to understand how workers feel … and adapt behavior accordingly.

Recognizing each person's value. Diversity is part of the value each person brings to a business. The specific talent, skill, or ability that individual adds to a team, department, or work group may be the single most valuable asset in solving a future business problem. The value of each person's individuality can be priceless if utilized.

Responsibility

Responsibility *entails recognition of our own biases and prejudices.* It also means remembering that we are not the center of the universe.

Being responsible in a working environment no longer simply means fulfilling job duties. Responsibility means:

> "It seems to me that any full grown, mature adult would have a desire to be responsible, to help where he can in a world that needs so very much, that threatens us so very much."
>
> Norman Lear
> U.S. American television producer

- Learning about others and respecting their views
- Exposing ourselves to new and different ways of doing things
- Eliminating our stereotypes in order to achieve mutually respectful and genuine relationships with others.

And remember, responsibility is a two-way street; we need to have both sides work on the issue. Think back in your life about how mattering and respect boosted your bottom line, increased positive work relationships, and was personally rewarding as well.

Pull Your Head Out of the Sand by Turning Marginalization into Mattering

What should you do to transform your marginalizing behaviors into mattering behaviors? Following is a chapter summary and a few suggestions of how you can take immediate action.

1   *Be self-aware of your biases, actions, and behaviors.* Be aware of your inner talk; ask yourself if you are operating on auto-pilot or if you are choosing to respond in that way. For a refresher course, revisit the techniques and end of chapter exercises in Chapters 2 and 3.

2   *Use inclusive language.* For example, when using pronouns, don't always use "he." Use "he" and "she" about equally, or use them both. Use plurals instead of singulars when that makes sense. Language and words have a lot of power; be sure you say what you mean.

3   *Reach out and support targeted individuals.* Give your support and show that you care when someone has been marginalized. You can talk with the person privately. You can also support their ideas and contributions in meetings. Give voice to your support.

4   *Work toward removing personal barriers that marginalize and disrespect people in the workplace.* Ask a person you respect and trust to help you by pointing out situations in which you treat others in a marginal way. For example, "I want to be sure I'm considering all opinions in this decision. If it seems like I'm not doing this, I want you to bring it to my attention."

5   *Maintain a respectful work environment free of offensive practices and conditions.* Remove environmental barriers that may exclude or marginalize others. (Yes, this means taking down the pin-up and body-builder calendars as

well as any other materials that could be judged to be offensive.)

6   *Look for the value and contribution of others.* Try this team activity:

   • Ask every member of your team to write down the greatest contributions each member personally makes to the team (patient, good problem-solver, detail-oriented, always asks tough questions). Also ask individuals to write down what they believe to be their own contributions.

   • Share results.
     Now ask: Do perceptions of self-value match those expressed by others?

   • Discuss what the impacts of individual contributions are on the team. (It feels great to be valued, increases my productivity, I was surprised to see what others consider to be my contribution.)

7   *Identify a time when you were marginalized or made to matter, and share your stories.* Stories can be powerful and transformational. They personalize a difficult topic, and help others develop empathy. Remember what it was like when you were invisible at the office or in the meeting, when it was expected that you could work odd hours because you were single, or when you were not asked to go out with the group because you were a single parent. Share these experiences with others and listen to their stories so you can better learn the impact of mattering and marginality on everyone around you.

8   *Own up to improper or inappropriate behavior.* Don't make excuses for an issue about your behavior that someone raises. Find a way to resolve these issues. Ask for help with your own "blind spots." Don't forget, you may not know what you don't know (remember the Johari Window?).

9 *Be aware of behaviors that may unintentionally marginalize others.* Monitor your own behavior. You can't change behavior if you aren't even aware of it. Ask others to bring it to your attention ... and then thank them instead of being defensive when they do.

10 *Be aware of the perspectives and needs of others with whom you work. Appreciate the differences.* If there's an issue arising over a difference, openly acknowledge it with the other person. Discuss the different perspectives and together choose how to proceed to reach a resolution.

11 *Be willing to give and receive appropriate feedback.* Try this exercise in a group setting:

- Appoint a facilitator (manager/supervisor/team lead) to observe this activity.
- Have participants pair up (have one group of three if necessary).
- The facilitator chooses a developmental area on which each participant can provide feedback (a strength/positive characteristic or opportunity for improvement, such as communication style, interaction with clients, behaviors in meetings, team approach, etc.).
- One person starts. Follow this process:
  a. State the constructive purpose of your feedback
  b. Describe specifically what you have observed
  c. Describe your reactions
  d. Give the other person the opportunity to respond
  e. Make other specific suggestions
  f. Summarize and express your support.
- Reverse the roles with the facilitator noting the interaction.
- Participants should practice using the process steps effectively while exhibiting the proper body language and tone. Make mental notes of specifics for the discussion following the experience.

- Following the exercise, the facilitator leads a discussion: "How did you feel during the exercise ... comments ... etc."

12 *Encourage open and frank communications by asking and listening.* If James seems to be holding back, give him permission to discuss his feelings openly by saying something like, "James, we'd like to hear what you think." Create space for him to speak. People need to give voice to their emotions and be heard and acknowledged by others.

13 *Compliment and encourage others on their contributions.* Some people think that complimenting someone causes them to slack off. Nonsense! Complimenting others demonstrates mattering behavior. Thanking people for their contributions encourages more of the same behavior.

14 *Confront inappropriate jokes, humor, language, or conversation.* But do it in a one-on-one, non-shaming, and respectful way. Depending on the situation, avoid confronting inappropriate behavior openly in a meeting as it may cause embarrassment and shut down the communication. People usually take feedback best when it's one-on-one, in a non-threatening situation, and delivered by someone who genuinely cares about the person and the outcome.

15 *Be clear in your communications about how you feel and what you want.* Getting constructive feedback depends on the words you use:

Word Sequence	Explanation
"When you ..."	*Start with a "When you ..." statement that describes the behavior without judgment, exaggeration, labeling, attribution, or motives. Just state the facts as specifically as possible.*
"I feel ..."	*State how the behavior affects you. If you need more than a word or two to describe the feeling, it is probably just some variation of joy, sorrow, anger, or fear.*
"Because I ..."	*Now say why you are affected that way. Describe the connection between the facts you observe and the feelings they provoke in you.*
(pause for discussion)	**Let the other person respond.**
"I would like ..."	*Describe the change you want the other person to consider ...*
"Because ..."	*... and why you think the change will alleviate the problem.*
"What do you think?"	*Listen to the other person's response. Be prepared to discuss options and compromise on a solution.*

Now practice being clear in your communications by stating feelings and wants. Use the above word sequence to describe a situation you would like to change:

Word Sequence	Explanation
"When you ..."	
"I feel ..."	
"Because I ..."	
(pause for discussion)	**Let the other person respond.**
"I would like ..."	
"Because ..."	
"What do you think?"	

16 *Write down two things you can do differently at work* to make certain that other employees or customers aren't marginalized:

1.

2.

Chapter 5

Broaden Your World View: See things as THEY are not as YOU are

"Most ignorance is vincible ignorance; we don't know because we don't want to know."

Aldous Huxley
English novelist, essayist

Being unaware of what another person needs can be the catalyst for harmful conflict and problems.

Consider the ostrich.

Proud. Noble. Protective. And never more protective than when it avoids conflict and danger by attempting to stick its head in the sand. It's cool there. Peaceful. But there's one huge drawback: it leaves an exposed, conspicuous rear end sticking up in the air.

Such is the cost of unawareness. It often seems easier to ignore or avoid a potentially difficult situation by keeping oneself in a position of ignorance or unawareness. Ignorance really is not bliss, as the adage states, but a state of being that is costly to personal relationships, and thus, the bottom line.

The successful employee cannot live and work in today's complex, multicultural world without sensitivity and awareness of the perspectives and needs of others. The costs are too great.

How do we remedy this lack of awareness?

- Assert personal responsibility.
- Engage in risk-taking.
- Capitalize on educational diversity experiences and opportunities.

Ethnocentrism vs. Geocentrism

A story ...

A man had lived in the same small town all his life, working to earn enough money for the only vacation he'd ever take — a trip around the world. He began saving money when he was a boy, putting away pennies that other children would have spent on candy and toys.

As he grew, he continued saving and began planning. His wife and family learned to make do with less because of "the big trip." Whenever the man felt downhearted, he'd think of the journey he someday would take around the world and his spirits would soar.

One day, after his children moved away and his wife died, the man finally took the trip he had saved for and planned for so many years. For months he traveled across the countries and landscapes he had dreamed of all his life.

> *"There is nowhere you can go and only be with people who are like you. Give it up."*
>
> Bernice Johnson Regon
> Musician and Curator, Community
> Life Division, Smithsonian Institute

When he returned, his friends gathered around him, waiting to hear stories of strange lands, exotic ports of call, and exciting people. "So, what was it like to see the world?" a friend asked.

The old man sighed and said, "Disappointing. It wasn't like home at all!"

The above story about the world traveler may be an oversimplification, but the point is well-taken. It is human nature to look at the world through one perspective and expect everyone else to have the same view. This tendency is called *"ethnocentrism"* or *"egocentrism."*

Ethnocentrism *holds that one's world view or beliefs are superior to those of other groups or cultures.* Pick something you have a strong belief about, such as what family should look like, religion, manners, etc. Have you ever seen yourself as better than others who don't share your same beliefs?

This monocultural view of the world can get us in real trouble in our work and interactions with others. Prejudice, bias, and stereotyping associated with ethnocentrism can seriously undermine our efforts to work with others who are different from us. This is especially true if others hold their own centric views of the world.

Truly egocentric people believe that others' beliefs and needs always come second to their own. One of the most damaging of the unsavory elements of ethnocentrism is the fact that, *by overvaluing our own beliefs and way of life, we're devaluing the lives of others.*

Sidebar, Your Honor!

We can't talk about ethnocentrism without mentioning its ugly cousin, internalized marginalization. Here's how one comedian evaluated it.

Internalized marginalization *is the tendency to claim that we and/or the group we belong to is being more oppressed or is at a greater disadvantage than any other person or group.* Just as the grass is always greener on the other side, it's easy to claim our grass is browner than another, more trampled upon.

The disadvantage of this activity is that time spent complaining about how weak or beaten down we are is time that COULD have been spent making strides on our own behalf and on behalf of others.

"Everybody's encouraged to be touchy. That is, everybody but me. I'm the White Anglo-Saxon male. Black people think I'm physically deficient and oppressive. Gay people think I'm latently homosexual and overly macho. Women think I'm oafish and horny. Asians think I'm lazy and stupid. You think YOU'VE got an axe to grind? I'm #@%ing Paul Bunyan!"*

Dennis Miller
U.S. American comedian

How Does Ethnocentrism Happen?

Ethnocentrism would seem to happen naturally wherever there are people with high self-esteem. What person or culture doesn't think they're better than someone else somewhere? Who doesn't believe they have the one best right way to get things done.

For example, which way should the toilet paper be hung? Over or under the roll? Do you instruct family members how to install the roll? Do you feel so passionate about the right way the paper should flow that you have actually changed it at a friend's house? And to think we're talking about something that has no impact on our lives really. Imagine applying this same principle to things that really matter.

> *"Culture is dictatorial unless understood and examined."*
>
> Edward T. Hall
> *Interculturalist, author*

Even people who pride themselves on "worldliness," fairness and openness to new ideas and experiences have an occasional bout of ethnocentrism. To remember what causes it, think of one of the most self-centered words in the English language, screamed at the top of your lungs —MEEEE!

Ethnocentrism usually happens when we're in our M.E.E.E.E. behaviors of being:

- *Mad* — When we're angry, it's easy to point fingers and blame others.

- *Embarrassed* — When our point of view is challenged, rather than admit that we lack understanding, we strongly and defensively adhere to our own point of view.

- *Exposed* — We feel as though our insecurities have been brought to the forefront and so we play on the insecurities of others.

- *Excluded* — We've had negative experiences by being excluded from the group.

- *Exhausted* — We're tired and frustrated with a situation. Our belief in our superiority is what consoles us and "recharges our battery."

People tend to be more forgiving and flexible when they're in a safe emotional place, and less forgiving when in any of the five states mentioned above. These opposing perspectives will often cause misunderstandings, miscommunications, and misapplied judgments on all sides.

You're in a sales meeting watching an exchange between a senior account rep and a junior account rep. The senior account rep says, "After 26 years of sales experience, I know how to get results." To which the junior sales rep replies, "The world is changing, we need to use new strategies to meet these new needs." Both statements are right yet both statements are wrong, reflecting an ethnocentric perspective.

How do we get past these feelings that lead us to ethnocentrism?

- *Become aware of our own tendency to judge the world from our perspective.* That's not hard. We do it naturally, constantly, and without provocation.

- *Realize that our view is not the only possible one in any given interaction or situation.* This may be the most difficult thing to learn to do. Realizing our way is not the only option does NOT mean we're wrong or did it wrong in the past. It simply means that, as the world changes, our options change, too.

- *Discard the notion that any other perspectives are wrong.* Which, of course, leads us to ...

- *Acknowledge that another perspective could help.* It can be a big relief to discover that someone unlike ourselves might actually give us the answer to questions or the solution to problems with which we are struggling.

- *Visualize other options.* What's the worst that would happen if I simply tried to understand other perspectives? Shift your perspective. Instead of judging, try to move to understanding.

By doing these things, you get out of your own "bubble" and see the world in a different way. By doing these things, you can start to arrive at a "geocentric" view.

Geocentrism — Our Hero

You're at the World's Fair and you're hungry. As you walk between the exhibits, you catch the aroma of some of the world's most mouth-watering cuisine. You start making lunch plans in your head.

"First I'll stop by the Chinese exposition hall for pot stickers. Then, it's off to the French pavilion for a little paté fois gras. A cup of Manhattan clam chowder would hit the spot at the United States exhibit, followed by some authentic German potato salad. Chicken tandoori from India would be the perfect main course. And for dessert, some baklava from Greece along with a dark steaming cup of Colombian coffee."

But when the food police (I know there's no such thing; just go with me on this one) find out you're from Scotland, they tell you you're only allowed to eat blood pudding and haggis. Sure, you like blood pudding and haggis. Who wouldn't? But why stick with the hometown dish when you've got so many other options at your fingertips?

Congratulations! Your stomach is practicing geocentrism.

Geocentrism *is the ability to find a variety of choices when seeing the world and situations.* The more you can broaden your collection of visions, the better you will be able to communicate successfully with employees and customers who are different from ourselves. This geocentric and non-judgmental view can be a valuable business skill that will have a positive impact on both our own productivity and the bottom line.

Let's look at some companies that are practicing geocentrism. Charles Schwab and IBM focus leadership development efforts on recruiting, developing and promoting women and minority managers. Schwab tracks many factors to ensure that women and minorities have equal promotional and developmental opportunities. IBM has 38% of its top management team made up of women, minorities and non-U.S. born people. Women hold top positions in Peru, Indonesia, France, Spain, Portugal, Singapore, Hong Kong, and Latin America.

Other organizations, such as Apple, AOL Time Warner, AT&T, Eddie Bauer, Ben & Jerry's and EDS support coaching, professional development and career planning for Asians, Hispanics, gays and lesbians. In addition, 76 of the Fortune 100 firms have nondiscrimination policies that include sexual orientation, and 44 offer domestic partner benefits to gay and lesbian employees.[1]

Moving Toward Geocentrism

Moving from an ethnocentric perspective to a geocentric world view is one of the most important business skills that you can acquire but it takes hard work. Try these tools:

- *Increased Awareness* — Take a close look at early learnings to figure out where you got your ethnocentric behaviors. Take a look at what you do unconsciously that you don't even know why.

  Imagine that you're at a friend's house for dinner. Before putting the roast in the oven, she cuts off both ends and throws away good meat. You ask, "Why did you do that?" She says, "I'm not sure, my mom always did it that way." You reply, "Let's find out why ... you paid good money for that roast!"

  The friend calls her mother, who has the same response, "I'm not sure, my mom always did it that way." Now the two of you are on a quest. Your friend calls across the country to talk to her grandma. Grandma exclaims, "You're doing what? I always cut the ends off because my pan was too small and the roast wouldn't fit in the roaster."

  How much have you thrown away in your life without thinking about it? How much have you discarded just because "that's the way it's always been done"?

- *Education* — Find out whatever you can about people and cultures that are different from your own. Worship with people of different faiths to learn about their spirituality and beliefs. Check the exercises at the end of Chapter 2 for more details.

- *Sort Old and New Information* — Decide which views you hold that are uninformed or out-of-date and which ones you want to keep as part of your belief system.

  For instance, learn about how other cultures use eye contact to communicate. Don't jump to the conclusion that Asians or Native Americans are hiding something simply because they don't readily look you in the eye.

- *Take Risks* — Put yourself in new, different, and uncomfortable situations and cultural experiences to narrow the boundaries of your ethnocentrism and expand your geocentric view. Get involved. Contact public institutions and officials to encourage their continued support of targeted groups.

- *Travel* — Traveling exposes you to many perspectives that you cannot learn simply by reading or watching TV ... but you have to be open to it.

  When my sister and I were traveling internationally, several demonstrations broke out in the country we were visiting. Our travel plans were altered as a result. Upon her return to Houston, her boss exclaimed in his ethnocentrism, "See what happens when you leave the great state of Texas!" Imagine the size of his world, and imagine all we learned from our new experiences.

  Sometimes seeing really is believing. Consider that the United States borders two countries with very different cultures. We can learn from the French-speaking Canadians that value their French roots and Spanish-speaking Mexicans with Spanish, Native American, and South American roots. Or just travel from Seattle, Washington to Birmingham, Alabama and experience the wonderful array of cultures within the United States.

Moving toward geocentrism means identifying and discarding old habits.

"I'm Only Human"
Common Mistakes
for Common People

Stereotypes (or "Hey, You're Not Like the REST of Them!")

Stereotyping *is when you see a person as member of a group and the information you have about that group is applied to that person.*

What's up with THAT?

Granted, there is an advantage to stereotyping — it makes our lives easier. It helps to make some sense of our world. It would be too difficult to try to sort out all of the information about people as individuals. It's easier to make broad generalizations, even though some may be ridiculous. After all, white men can't jump. Of course, for that to be true, we'd have to ignore the athletic contributions of Larry Bird, John Stockton, Kevin McHale, and Pete Maravich.

By identifying when we stereotype, we can avoid doing it inappropriately. We stereotype when:

> "*Every person is, in many respects, like all other people, like some other people, like no other person.*"
>
> *C. Kluckhohn and H.A. Murray*
> *Editors, Personality in Nature,*
> *Culture and Society*

- *We lack information about certain groups.* The less knowledge we have about them, the more we tend to use stereotypes to fill in the voids.

- *We have little or no connection with members of different groups.* The fewer experiences we have, the more we tend to fall back on our stereotypes, particularly if the one person we know from that group happens to fit the stereotype.

"So What If We Stereotype? It's Human Nature, Right?"

Yes, it's natural to stereotype. But it does have its pitfalls, especially in the workplace. Stereotyping can:

- *Keep us from fully recognizing and valuing all that a person brings to the table.* For example, seeing a physical disability before seeing the person can unfairly limit that individual's contributions.

- *Cause us to make untrue and/or unfair assumptions about others.* It can cause us to judge them as somehow inferior or flawed, as in, "He's wrong for this job. His style is too loud, too aggressive, almost hostile."

- *Prevent someone from getting hired.* "They don't work as hard." "They're lazy." Or "They've got too many family responsibilities to really care about their job."

- *Determine a person's role in an organization.* For instance, "I know her background is in finance, but she is Chinese. She must speak Chinese so she would be a great asset in our Chinatown branch as the PR person."

- *Hinder career mobility.* For instance, "Asians are good workers, but not management material." Another example that is still all too real is the proportionately small ratio of women to men at the highest levels of U.S. American organizations.

- *Cause job separation.* Members of certain groups are segregated into certain job functions in organizations. Consider the number of African American executives in Affirmative Action/EEO and diversity positions.

So, yes, stereotyping DOES matter. For organizations, it's also very costly when you consider the amount of talent that is underutilized or, worse yet, goes unrecognized!

Bias and Prejudice

Certain biases or prejudicial attitudes just seem to be built into our world views or perspectives. These opinions form a part of the way people are socialized into the world. Prejudice is the result of pre-judging, which we do in most situations to analyze what we are facing. However, if a certain bias or prejudice causes us to behave in a way that marginalizes another person, we need to eliminate that behavior.

> *"Our prejudices are like physical infirmities — we cannot do what they prevent us from doing."*
>
> John Lancaster Spalding
> Bishop Emeritus of Peoria, author

Companies are realizing the effect these marginalizing behaviors are having on the bottom line, on worker productivity, and in creating workplace tension between employees. Companies cannot change attitudes or beliefs but they can — and do — regulate behaviors. In doing so, they are requiring individuals to treat every other employee with respect.

Awareness of our own biases and prejudicial attitudes is a key element in creating a workplace free of marginalizing behaviors. It is up to each employee to act in ways that make others matter and are respectful of their individuality.

> *"In overcoming prejudice, working together is even more effective than talking together."*
> Ralph W. Sockman
> Senior Minister of Christ Church, Methodist, NYC, author

Importance of Discomfort

Discomfort from confrontation can provide great growth. If you're not experiencing any resistance, you're not moving forward. A little discomfort can be a positive sign.

Did you ever learn to play a musical instrument or take up a new sport? In the beginning there was an adjustment period, a time of discomfort, sore muscles, aching fingers, or a headache from too much new information. You thought about throwing in the towel ... but you're glad you didn't. It was worth going through an awkward, "uncomfortable" period in order to enjoy the eventual payoff.

Moving from ethnocentrism to geocentrism is a similar journey. For many, it may cause some discomfort. But remember:

> *"If something makes me uncomfortable, or scares me, I have to surround myself with it and get to understand its shape. Then it can't affect me."*
> David Wojnarowicz
> U.S. American artist, writer

Feeling uncomfortable is a natural part of both the change and growth processes. If you don't go through a little discomfort, chances are you're neither changing nor growing.

Learning about others and grappling with issues of diversity can often be a new experience, making some feel ill at ease. But if we take the risk and put ourselves in these uncomfortable situations, we have the potential for great change and growth.

The world and the workplace are both rapidly changing environments. The individuals who will thrive in these environments are the ones who:

- Stay abreast of any changes
- Manage the changes in their own lives
- Use change as a method for growth and improvement.

The people who put forth the effort to follow these guidelines will be successful, productive, and well-adjusted employees — the kind of people every company needs.

Pull Your Head Out of the Sand by Broadening Your World View

What should you do to broaden your world view? Following is a chapter summary and a few suggestions of how you can take immediate action.

1   *Recognize your own stereotypes.* Identify specific people or groups of people that you often niche into characterized stereotypes. Now think about how or where you first formed your opinions about that group or groups. What were you taught by your parents? What did you learn from your friends? Did movies and television influence your opinion? What sources contributed and/or contribute to reinforcing your stereotypes?

2   *Do a self-assessment that gives you a snapshot of where you are today in terms of your knowledge and understanding about others who are different from you.* None of us is free from bias. But we must work to know when we are *unfairly* judging another based on stereotypes or bias. So ...

   •   Identify what you tend to judge others on (dress, age, gender, etc.) that can negatively impact your view of them.

   •   Jot down when and where your attitudes about others have had an impact on them in a negative way.

   •   Review your findings with someone you trust.

   •   What behaviors are evident to the other person that confirm your biases and stereotypes?

3   *Test your assumptions about others.* Collect more information about others before you make decisions that could affect your working relationship(s). Just because you can't see the stars during the day doesn't mean they aren't shining.

4   *Find or create opportunities to connect with people different from you.* Invite someone to lunch whom you ordinarily would not ask. Join a different group for an after-work social activity. Get information from organizations that can give you history, culture, challenges and contributions of certain groups (e.g., Council on American-Islamic Relations). Attend diversity events and mingle with those from a diverse group.

5   *Be willing to feel others' discomfort now and then.* You can't grow if you don't risk a little discomfort. Try to make connections with others on an emotional level. Have conversations where the goal is to learn to recognize and understand why others feel as they do. Try to perceive how it feels to "walk their way."

6   *Ask the person you've made assumptions about, "What makes you tick?"* Most people are not offended that you want to know more about them if you do it in a genuine manner.

7   *Consider your world view.* Do others see what you see? Below is an image of an oak tree. What does an oak tree mean to you? Now answer from the view of:

A child …

An artist …

A real estate agent …

A dog …

Do you all see the same thing?

Just ask the dog!

8   *Consider what you lose.* Think of all the opportunities we miss when we don't test our assumptions about others. We run the risk of NOT hiring the best person for the job, NOT promoting the best person for the position, or lose the potential to build a great new relationship that might expand our own world view and enrich us personally.

9   *Reinforcing the right behaviors leads to the right results.* Reinforcing and complimenting an individual's behaviors will encourage the same behaviors next time.

10 *Write down two things you can do differently at work* that put the concepts in this chapter into action:

1.

2.

Chapter 6

Which Way Out of the Desert?
Progress is made with just one step

"The man who removes a mountain begins
by carrying away small stones."

Chinese proverb

Do Something! ... Anything!

The work papers are stacked on your desk. Everybody wants it done now. Deadlines are looming like children around a birthday cake. There's work to be done. Lots of it.

What do you do?

Nothing.

Unfortunately, that's an easy and fairly common reaction when faced with an overwhelming task or series of tasks. The same holds true when it comes to diversity.

Feeling personally overwhelmed by everything you need to know and understand around diversity issues is common. However, letting it prevent you from doing anything at all will merely compound the problem.

At one point in my life I was overwhelmed, struggling with making a major life decision, so I began praying for a sign from God telling me what I should do. The next day, I rounded a street corner to see a marquis in bold capital letters, "If you're waiting for a sign from God ... this is it." I nearly drove onto the curb!

If you're feeling overwhelmed and struggling with the prospect of all this diversity work, maybe, like it was for me, the sign you've been waiting for is right in front of you and you don't even see it. So, perhaps it's time to take small, manageable action steps, and not wait any longer.

Cut Me Some Slack!

Gladly. Here goes:

We probably never will become perfect with regard to all the multicultural and diversity issues in the world and workplace. But we can become proficient at some things.

It is the sense of competence in learning about things that, one step at a time, will give us the resolve and courage to continue to learn more. The old adage, "Yard by yard, life is hard. But inch by inch, life's a cinch," is apt in describing the growing sensitivity to diversity issues. Don't be overwhelmed by the "yards" of diversity information you may need to learn. Learn just one inch each day, and the yard will take care of itself.

If Not Now, When?

What do you do when you arrive at work? Pour yourself a cup of coffee? Glance at the newspaper? Begin responding to voice mail and e-mail? Get down to business? Chances are, the last thing you'd do is plan out what you can do throughout the day to promote diversity in the workplace.

It's okay. You can be honest. It won't hurt my feelings.

Let's face it. It would seem that there's never a good time to make changes or to devote time to promoting and developing an appreciation of diversity in the workplace. The excuses are many and, at first glance, quite solid.

"I'm burnt out! I don't have the enthusiasm for it."

"I'm doing more with less at work as it is!"

"Who has time?"

"There's nothing in it for me."

Diversity issues impose themselves on our already over-worked lives, and you are now expected to learn more about interculturalism. When will it all end? Predictably, you want to throw up your hands in dismay and give up because you can't know everything there is to know and do everything that needs to be done.

So, what do you do when you see a heaping helping of diversity issues being added to your already full plate of workday tasks? One suggestion is to look at all the other helpings on the plate and see the diversity component already in each portion. This might resolve some of that sense of being overwhelmed.

A Positive Spin

Feeling defensive and acting defiant when confronted with diversity challenges merely sets up win/lose situations. If you resent diversity issues, you will unnecessarily add to your frustration since you'll be fighting battles that don't need to be fought. When frustrated, you can easily marginalize others. Instead, put that energy to use in more productive ways. It will take a lot less effort simply to be open to learning about the diversity of others. In fact, taken in the proper context, the learning can be both beneficial and enjoyable.

Honoring ... Beyond Acceptance

Acceptance includes the concept of respect. In order to accept something, you first need to respect it. Honoring goes beyond this and implies that you value the things you respect and accept. Your greatest rewards will come when you reach for — and incorporate into your life — the value gained from the things you respect and accept.

> *"We may have come over on different ships, but we're all in the same boat now."*
>
> *Whitney Young, Jr.*
> *Author, Former Director,*
> *National Urban League*

No one knows it all with regard to diversity. But now you know enough to make a difference in yourself and where you work. The task becomes less overwhelming if you keep in mind some simple ideas:

- *Each of us can accept the personal responsibility to learn more.* The most important work that can occur around diversity issues is that of personal responsibility and education.

- *Pointing fingers at others will get us nowhere.* Assigning blame only arouses anger and defensive behaviors in others.

- *The only change we can really control is the change we decide to make in ourselves.* This change will most often occur through educational experiences and by becoming involved with uncomfortable situations where we are learning new information.

If we are to have a better world, it will start with a personal commitment of self-accountability and ongoing education.

Pull Your Head Out of the Sand by Taking That First Step

What steps can you take that will help lead you out of the vast desert of diversity issues? Following is a chapter summary and a few suggestions of how you can take immediate action.

1   *If you experience a difficult "diversity moment," see it as an opportunity to learn more about yourself and others.* Reframe the experience and take three big steps:

   a. Stop and ask, "What is going on here?" Look at the big picture. Listen to your internal chitchat, and identify the kinds of judgments you are making about others. How might your attitude contribute to making this a difficult situation?

   b. Take time to consider how others are viewing the situation. Ask them for feedback about how they see the situation.

   c. Try to resolve the issue together. The goal is for all parties to be open to learning how each perceives the situation and do some collaborative problem solving.

2   *Unclutter your mind.* Put aside your judgments and seek information to assess things from a clearer perspective. It's a busy day, you're frazzled, and the day's events are cluttering your mind. Take a time out. Go for a walk. Clear your head. If no one's life is at stake, wait until morning to make a decision.

3   *Make a personal connection.* Make it a personal mission to establish a relationship with someone from a targeted group. Show that you can build an inclusive community.

4   *Do a reality check with someone you trust.* Get some feedback on your behavior. Learn to recognize how your behavior makes an impact on others.

5   *Take personal responsibility.* You have choices when
    reacting to situations. The more you are aware of your
    choices, the more responsibility you take for your actions.
    Personal responsibility can take the form of respect for
    others, being there for others, and assisting them to do
    their job successfully. This means being open and
    forthright with others, giving them feedback when
    necessary, and being open to receiving feedback from
    them. The act of inclusion, making sure that people in
    your work group feel that they are part of the team, is
    just as important. It is through each of these principles
    that you can help to create an equitable and trusting
    workplace.

6   *Re-examine your beliefs objectively.* Of course, you have a
    right to your beliefs. However, consider how they may
    translate into actions that may pose barriers for others
    who do not share your values.

7   *Acknowledge that others may be feeling overwhelmed as well.*
    Most people shy away from speaking publicly about
    diversity except in diversity training. Or they'll make fun
    of diversity when an opportunity presents itself. Part of
    diversity work is being able to recognize that it touches us
    in every aspect of our lives and that it is not only
    appropriate but healthy to discuss issues of difference
    with one another openly and honestly.

8   *Create your own personal learning community.* A learning
    community is a group of trusted members with specific
    goals for development. It is a safe place to explore new
    ideas, perspectives, and ways of doing things. You may
    choose to set up a learning community with trusted
    colleagues in the workplace or in your community with
    family and neighbors. The key to success is to be
    intentional about becoming more conscious of human
    diversity.

9 *Create your own action plan.* Ultimately, diversity is about *choice.* You can choose to ignore all that you have learned about yourself and others, or you can begin to make a difference and engage in the diversity process by setting specific goals. Identify at least three things you want to work on, determine what you will need to accomplish your goals, set a timeline, and get going. Remember, change comes from action!

Goal	Steps to Accomplish	Timeframe	Resources Needed
1.			
2.			
3.			

10 *Write down two things you can immediately start doing at work* that will keep you from feeling overwhelmed by diversity issues:

1.

2.

Additional Notes

It's Now Up to You!

Hey, what's that sound?

Th ... tha ... tha–*woopf!*

Hooray! One more diversity-challenged ostrich has successfully pulled its head out of the sand. Was it you?

There's a good chance it *was* you if you have read each chapter and completed at least some of the end of chapter action items in this book. Congratulations! And thank you for sticking with it. I know it wasn't ALL easy.

As you strut out of the desert with your head held high and eyes wide open, conduct yourself in a manner that demonstrates that you understand the key diversity concepts to building effective relationships outlined in this book.

1 *Stop Walking On Eggshells: Define and use positive confrontation.* You know that you directly influence how your relationships are developed and shaped. You have the tools to develop effective relationships with those of different cultures or abilities. You can stop walking on eggshells by taking risks, appropriately confronting difficult situations, and managing conflict. Once you do, you will benefit from strong, healthy relationships that can help you reach both personal and professional goals.

2 *I'm Okay, But "They" Need Help: Why should I change?* You can identify the personal rewards you gain by implementing personal change. Using the head, heart, and hand model will help make you more aware of the things you say and do. Remember this model emphasizes that, in every situation, you choose your response. By recognizing your ability to change outcomes, and by making different response choices, you can begin to experience the benefits of those changes.

3   *Help Others Matter: Unleash the power of diversity.* You are either included or excluded by others, which causes you to feel and behave in certain ways. You also include or exclude others. Individuals who feel they are being excluded often respond with less motivation and productivity. You have the power to change that response by choosing words and actions that make others feel they matter.

4   *Broaden Your World View: See things as they are not as you are.* You have had an opportunity to identify some of your biases, prejudices, and stereotypical ideas of others; we are all somewhat ethnocentric. It's part of being human. Acknowledging and admitting to these negative social forces strengthens your relationships with others, improves the bottom line, and enhances your potential to advance along your career path.

5   *Which Way Out Of The Desert: Progress is made with just one step.* Make a commitment. Take one tiny step forward. Take another. How about one more? Before long you'll discover you're a long way from where you started. When it comes to making changes the important thing is to just start. Risk-taking and moving into discomfort will move you away from a limiting view of the world and toward a broader, more enriching view. The goal is to overcome unconscious acts of exclusion and build more effective relationships.

I hope you'll keep this little book on a nearby shelf to review and use as a quick reference from time to time. And, now that you're on your way out of the desert, why stop there? I've included a bibliography of other resources that can broaden your knowledge and introduce you to the limitless rewards of learning to navigate within this diverse world.

In closing, remember that it takes a strong personal commitment to change behavior; that behavior change will reap benefits in every aspect of your life. It's now up to you.

A. S. Tolbert, Ph.D.

About the Author

Amy S. Tolbert, Ph.D., is a consultant and trainer in the areas of human resources and organization development. She is a principal of Effecting Creative Change in Organizations (ECCO International), which specializes in creating a new sense of spirit and preparing people and organizations for sustainability in an ever-changing environment.

Addressing diversity and multicultural issues, cross-cultural training, and managing a diverse workforce, Dr. Tolbert has co-authored and presented the "Discovering Diversity Profile," a popular self-assessment tool, at the American Society for Training and Development (ASTD) International Conference and the Inscape Publishing (formerly Carlson Learning Company) International Conference. She has presented nationally and internationally at the International Human Resource Development Organization Conference; the International Management Development Organization; the "Quality Workforce for the Year 2000," a national conference co-sponsored by ASTD; and other national conferences. She also co-developed the "Integrating Diversity Profile," which assesses key areas for organizations to focus their time and energies regarding diversity efforts.

Dr. Tolbert consults and trains nationally in the areas of international training and development, e-learning/business television design and production, persuasive presentation/communication skills, managing within a diverse workforce, motivation and leadership skills. Her diverse client list includes 3M, Best Buy, Mayo Clinic, and the United Way.

Diverse experiences take Dr. Tolbert from the United States to Latin America, from Fortune 100 companies to non-profits and, from the cold winter climate of her home state of Minnesota to warm sunny climates whenever possible. Although she has many accomplishments, she considers her marriage and two inspiring daughters to be at the top of the list.

Dr. Tolbert received her doctorate in Human Resource Development, specializing in international/cross-cultural and diversity education and training, from the University of Minnesota.

For more information about Dr. Tolbert or ECCO International services, visit:

www.ECCOInternational.com

or email her at: amy@ECCOInternational.com.

Notes

Chapter 3: I'm Okay But "They" Need Help: Why should I change?

1   Lopez Negrete, A. (2000, September). The Hispanic Market
    Continues to Grow Everywhere! *Multicultural Marketing Resources
    (MMR) Newsletter.*
    Retrieved September 5, 2001, from
    http://www.inforesources.com/news/articles/art00sept.html

2   Cornitcher, D. & Skriloff, L. (1999, August). Multicultural
    Marketing: A Marketing Imperative. *Multicultural Marketing
    Resources (MMR) Newsletter.*
    Retrieved September 5, 2001, from
    http://inforesources.com/news/articles/art99aug.html

3   Johnson, D. W. & Johnson, F. P. (2000). *Joining together: Group
    theory and group skills* (7th ed., Chapter 10). Boston: Allyn & Bacon.

4   Judy, R. W. & D'Amico, C. (1999). *Workforce 2020: Work and workers
    in the 21st Century.* Indianapolis: Hudson Institute.

5   U.S. Department of Labor statistics.

6   Statistics from Women's Enterprise Web site.
    Retrieved October 31, 2001, from
    http://www.womens-enterprise.com/adv.html

7   *Gay Customers. Best Customers. $450 Billion.*
    Retrieved October 31, 2001, from
    http://www.planetoutpartners.com/PlanetOutPartnersSalesKit.pdf

8   KPMG LLP Consulting, New York. (2000, July).
    Retrieved on November 26, 2001, from
    http://usserve.us.kpmg.com/news_eventsnews/pr000725.htm

9   *World Development Indicators 2001,* World Bank. (2001).
    Retrieved on November, 26, 2001, from
    http://www.worldbank.org/data/databytopic/bullets.pdf

10 Mann, R.A. & Roberts, B.S. (n.d.) Sexual Harassment in the
    Workplace: A Primer.
    Retrieved on November 3, 2001, from
    http://www.uakron.edu/lawrev/robert1.html

11 D'Ancona & Pflaum, LLC (2000, February 14). Government Reports a 300+
    Percent Increase in Discrimination Lawsuits. *HR Watch.*
    Retrieved November, 2001, from
    http://hr.monster.com/hrwatch/2000/02/14/

12 *Sources for list of lawsuit figures:*

    • Denny's
    Press release (1999, August 26).
    Retrieved on November 26, 2001, from
    http://www.igc.org/tcrp/press/Discrimination/dennysone.htm

    • Home Depot
    News item post.
    Retrieved on November 26, 2001, from
    http://www.sgdblaw.com/past_cases.htm

    • Texaco and Coca-Cola
    Winter, G. (2000, November 17). Coca-Cola Settles Racial Bias Case.
    The New York Times.

    • Ford Motor Co.
    (2001, December 19). Ford Motor Co.: $10.5 million settles claims of reverse
    discrimination. *Chicago Tribune,* p. 2.

    • Microsoft
    Prencipe, L. W. (2001, April 27). Guarding Against Discrimination
    Lawsuits. *Infoworld.*
    Retrieved November, 2001, from
    http://www.infoworld.com/articles/ca/xml/01/04/30/
    010430calist.xml

13 Luft, J. (1984). *Group processes: An introduction to group dynamics*
    (3rd ed.). Palo Alto, CA: National Press Books.

Chapter 5: Broaden Your World View: See things as THEY are not as YOU are.

1   Koonce, R. (2001, December). Redefining Diversity. *Training and Development Magazine*, pp. 22-33.

Bibliography

Alba, R. D. (1990). *Ethnic identity: The transformation of white America*. New York: Yale University Press.
    Landmark study which examines the changing role of ethnicity in the lives of U.S. Americans from a broad range of European backgrounds and how those European Americans differentiate themselves from other racial minorities from Asia, Latin America and the Caribbean.

Allen, J. (1990). *I saw what you did and I know who you are*. Tucker, GA: Performance Management Publications.
    This easy read focuses on giving and receiving feedback. You will discover effective ways to give positive reinforcement to others in the workplace.

Allen, R. (2002). *Guiding change journeys*. San Francisco: Jossey-Bass Pfeiffer.
    A theory-to-practice workbook, the author offers eight exciting change journeys to help readers become authentic and well-rounded practitioners of change.

Boyett, J. H. & Conn, H. P. (1992). *Workplace 2000: The revolution reshaping American business*. New York: Plume.
    Documents the changes occurring in the workplace and the challenges and responses of business; case studies from successful corporations, including Motorola, Sara Lee, and Wal-Mart.

Brandon, S. G. (Ed.) (1978). *Dictionary of comparative religions*. New York: Macmillan.
    This volume thoroughly defines anthropology, iconography, philosophy, and the psychology of primitive and ancient, Asian and Western religions. Articles describe practices and philosophies of specific religions.

Cooperrider, D. (Ed.), Yaeger, T. F., Sorenson, P. F. (Ed.), & Whitney, D. (Ed.) (2000). *Appreciative inquiry: Rethinking human organization toward a positive theory of change*. Champaign, IL: Stipes Publishing LLC.
    This book helps build both a practical and research foundation for appreciative inquiry (AI) work. This enlightening collection of papers helps us use AI to build our new realities together and use our full potential.

Cose, E. (1995). *A man's world: How real is male privilege and how high is its price?* New York: Harper Collins.
    Reporting on the discontent and confusion men are feeling as changing gender roles and expectations challenge the core of male identity through use of interviews, historical context, reportage, and analysis.

Covey, S. R. (1996). *The seven habits of highly effective people*. New York: Simon & Schuster.
    A "principle-centered" program that will help put readers on the path to lasting personal satisfaction and achievement.

Cross, E. Y., Miller, F. A. (Ed.), & Seashore, E. W. (Ed.) (1994). *The promise of diversity: Over 40 voices discuss strategies for eliminating discrimination in organizations.* New York: Irwin Professional Publishing for NTL Institute.
A contemporary, future-focused business anthology that helps readers understand and address the often-controversial, always complex issues surrounding workplace diversity, discrimination, and change management.

Friskopp, A. & Silverstein, S. (1996). *Straight jobs, gay lives: Gay and lesbian professionals, the Harvard Business School, and the American workplace.* New York: Simon & Schuster Trade.
In-depth research study from interviews with Harvard Business School lesbian/ gay alumni about experiences in the workplace. Includes listings of companies with nondiscrimination policies and domestic partner benefits as well as gay employee groups and nationwide professional groups.

Gardenswartz, L. & Rowe, A. (1993). *Managing diversity: A complete desk reference and planning guide.* San Diego: Pfeiffer & Co.
Comprehensive, practical, indexed guide with activities, charts, and worksheets.

Goleman, D. (1995). *Emotional intelligence: Why it can matter more than IQ.* New York: Bantam.
Drawing from groundbreaking brain and behavioral research, Goleman shows the factors at work when people of high IQ flounder and those of modest IQ do well. These factors add up to a different way of being smart — "emotional intelligence." Emotional intelligence is not fixed at birth, and the author shows how its vital qualities can be nurtured and strengthened in everyone.

Graves, E. G. (1997). *How to succeed in business without being white: Straight talk on making it in America.* New York: HarperBusiness.
Founder and publisher of Black Enterprise magazine offers lessons and advice for succeeding in the corporate world.

Gray, J. (1992). *Men are from Mars, women are from Venus.* New York: Harper Collins.
A guide for understanding female-male relationships and the differences between the sexes. Advice on how to counteract differences in communication styles, emotional needs, and modes of behavior.

Hacker, A. (1992). *Two nations: Black and white, separate, hostile, unequal.* New York: Ballatine Books.
An analysis of a divided society and why racial disparities persist through the meaning of racism, conflicting theories of superiority and equality, as well as such subtle factors as guilt and sexual fears.

Hall, E. T. (1976). *Beyond culture.* New York: Anchor Press/Doubleday.
In this work, Hall helps the reader hold up a mirror to see the powerful grip of unconscious culture. In this self-discovery process, we see how culturally-determined, unconscious attitudes impact our thoughts, feelings, communication, and behaviors.

Harris, P. R. & Moran, R. T. (1991). *Managing cultural differences: High-performance strategies for a new world of business.* Houston: Gulf Publishing.
An encyclopedic array of advice, case materials and examples of competing successfully in the global marketplace, including specific cultural traits of European, Japanese, Middle Eastern, African, and Hispanic societies.

Helgesen, S. (1995). *The female advantage: Women's ways of leadership.* New York: Doubleday/Currency.
Research study with findings about the unique nature of female leadership through inclusive organizational forms, communications methods, and recognition of employee relationships. Four theories of leadership are studied with examples and business cases.

Hofstede, G. (1984). *Cultures consequences.* Newbury Park, CA: Sage Publications.
This book identifies the differences in thinking and action between people of 40 different countries. It identifies four key dimensions in which value systems are ordered which impacts thinking and behavior.

Hultman, K. & Gellerman, B. (2002). *Balancing individual and organizational values: Walking the tightrope to success.* San Francisco: Jossey-Bass/Pfeiffer.
This book explores the major value challenges confronting today's organizations and offers a systematic approach for revitalizing institutions through growth values.

Hultman, K. (1998). *Making change irresistible: Overcoming resistance to change in your organization.* Palo Alto, CA: Davies-Black Publishing.
A practical step-by-step method for building trust, increasing team effectiveness, and helping employees adapt to the fast-paced change in today's workplace. Intended for executives, managers, and organizational consultants.

Johnson, D. W. & Johnson, F. P. (2000). *Joining together: Group theory and group skills* (7th ed.). Boston: Allyn & Bacon.
This book introduces readers to the theory and research findings needed to understand how to make groups effective, the role of trust, and the skills required to apply that knowledge in practical situations.

Johnston, W. B. & Packer, A. E. (1987). *Workforce 2000: Work and workers for the 21st Century.* Indianapolis: The Hudson Institute.
Landmark study and analysis of the changing U.S. American workforce. Hypothesized that changes in the 1980s U.S. American culture would result in a radically different USA by the year 2000, reshaping the economy, the workforce, and the workers.

Judy, R. W. & D'Amico, C. (1999). *Workforce 2020: Work and workers in the 21st Century.* Indianapolis: Hudson Institute.
A vision of the future U.S. American workforce prepared with the help of skilled economists, education experts, and policy researchers at Hudson Institute. A sequel to Workforce 2000.

Kanellos, N. (1996). *The Hispanic American almanac* (2nd ed.). New York: Gale Group.
Surveys Hispanic life and culture and assesses the impact of Hispanics on U.S.
history with chapters on Hispanic identity, language, religion, immigration
patterns, and the family.

Kanter, R. M. (1997). *World class: Thriving locally in the global economy.* New York: Touch-
stone.
Gaining local benefits from global opportunities through understanding the
impact of globalization on businesses, organizations, and individuals. Offers
excellent arguments and real-life examples.

Kivel, P. (1996). *Uprooting racism: How white people can work for racial justice.* Philadelphia:
New Society Publishers.
Designed to help white people act on their conviction that racism is wrong with
stories, suggestions, advice, exercises, and approaches for working together to
fight racism.

Lancaster, L. C. & Stillman, D. (2002). *When generations collide: Who they are. Why they clash.
How to solve the generational puzzle at work.* New York: Harper Collins.
This insightful book shows how to gain a new understanding of workplace
generational issues among traditionalists, baby boomers, generation xers, and
millennials.

Luft, J. (1969). *Of human interaction.* Palo Alto, CA: National Press Books.
The author explores a basic framework of the communication processes that
take place through a variety of human interactions.

Luft, J. (1984). *Group processes: An introduction to group dynamics* (3rd ed.). Palo Alto, CA:
National Press Books.
An introduction to the foundation of group processes. It explores the Johari
Window, basic issues, patterns, behaviors, psychological aspects, and current
trends.

Mendez-Russell, A., Wilderson Jr., F. R., & Tolbert, A. S. (1994). *Discovering diversity profile.*
Minneapolis: Inscape Publishing.
This self-scoring profile guides employees through a journey of self-discovery as
they respond to questions in four key areas: knowledge, understanding,
acceptance, and behavior. There is an accompanying facilitator's kit which
includes a technical manual, full and half-day seminar scripts, handouts and
overheads/PPTs for the seminars.

NTL Institute for Applied Behavioral Science. (1999). *Reading book for human relations
training* (8th ed.). Alexandria, VA: Author and others.
This compilation of readings provides theoretical and practical information, as
well as models, on communications, diversity, conflict, re-entry, self-awareness,
group dynamics, and learning.

Reina, D. S. & Reina, M. L. (1999). *Trust and betrayal in the workplace.* San Francisco: Berrett-
Koehler Publishers, Inc.
This book describes the ways that trust in the workplace can enhance worker
productivity and increase an employee's willingness to take risks, share informa-

tion, and learn from mistakes. It argues that, without trust, contemporary organizations will be unable to take the risks necessary to succeed in the rapidly changing environments of the new global economy.

Rhinesmith, S. H. (1996). *A manager's guide to globalization: Six skills for success in a changing world.* Chicago: Irwin.
One of the landmark studies of business and globalization based on the training of 5,000 managers from 35 countries. Outlines the six mindsets, characteristics, and management skills needed by managers to operate in a global organization.

Schlossberg, N. K., Waters, E. B., & Goodman, J. (1995). *Counseling adults in transition: Linking practice with theory* (2nd ed.). New York: Springer.
The authors combine an understanding of adult development with strategies for counseling clients in personal and professional transition. A framework is provided for individual, group, and work settings. The important diversity concept of marginalization is addressed.

Seashore, C. (1999). *What did you say? The art of giving and receiving feedback.* Columbia, MD: Bingham House Books.
This engaging book can be of use to anyone who has to offer or receive feedback from others. Author addresses why feedback tells more about the giver than the receiver through examples and vignettes. The struggle to understand each other is analyzed.

Senge, P. M. (1990). *The fifth discipline.* New York: Doubleday.
The Fifth Discipline has turned the principles of the learning organization into a movement of snowballing size and strength. This book explains that the ability to respond to change is a crucial issue, but management tools, such as "reengineering" and "total quality" simply treat the symptoms. It emphasizes systems thinking.

Senge, P. M. (Ed.), Cambron McCabe, N. H., Lucas, T., Kleiner, A., Dutton, J., & Smith, B. (2000). *Schools that learn: The fifth discipline fieldbook for everyone who cares about education.* New York: Doubleday.
A step-by-step guide on how to build a learning organization in your own company. This participative book offers tools, techniques, exercises, ideas, and stories to help put Senge's revolutionary theories into practice.

Shapiro, J. P. (1993). *No pity: People with disabilities forging a new civil rights movement.* New York: Times Books.
The story of the political awakening of the disability movement from the 17th Century deaf communities on Martha's Vineyard to the enactment of the Americans with Disabilities Act of 1992. Includes personal stories representing 43 U.S. Americans with disabilities.

Takai, R. (Ed.) (1990). *Strangers from a different shore: A history of Asian Americans.* New York: Penguin.
An extraordinary blend of narrative history, personal recollections, and oral testimony. A panoramic history of Asian-Americans from the Chinese who laid tracks for the transcontinental railroads, to plantation laborers in the cane fields of Hawaii, to present day challenges of assimilation and racism.

Tanenbaum, J. (1990). *Male and female realities: Understanding the opposite sex.* Costa Mesa, CA: Tanenbaum Assoc.
Exploration of male and female approaches to communication, sex, emotions, decisions, priorities, commitment, learning, and frames of reference. Suggestions are included on communicating and relating across gender differences.

Tannen, D. (2001). *You just don't understand: Women and men in conversation.* New York: Quill.
The complexities of communication between men and women coming from two different cultures and learned behavioral patterns.

Thomas, R. R., Jr. (1996). *Redefining diversity.* New York: Amacon.
An argument that diversity is more than an affirmative action or human resource issue. Presents a model titled the "diversity paradigm" that offers eight options for action.

Trompenaars, F. (1994). *Riding the waves of culture: Understanding diversity in global business.* Chicago: Irwin.
Helps U.S. corporations make the transition to maximize global business opportunities by adapting to new markets' local characteristics, legislation, fiscal regime, socio-political systems, and cultural systems. One of the landmark models in globalization.

Vaill, P. B. (1996). *Learning as a way of being.* San Francisco: Jossey-Bass.
A thoughtful critique of the roots of management education and argues that, if managers are to navigate the waters skillfully, institutions of "higher learning" must, above all, teach managers how to integrate the discipline of learning into their very being.

Weatherford, J. (1988). *Indian givers: How the Indians of the Americas transformed the world.* New York: Fawcett Columbine.
A leading anthropologist traces the crucial contributions made by Native Americans to the federal system of government, democratic institutions, modern medicine, agriculture, architecture, and ecology.

Winfeld, L. & Spielman, S. (1995). *Straight talk about gays in the workplace: Creating an inclusive, productive environment for everyone in your organization.* New York: Amacon.
Research showing that companies with progressive policies toward gays gain increased productivity, a better public image, and higher profitability; also shows the harmful effects of homophobia.

Zemke, R., Raines, C., & Filipczak, B. (2000). *Generations at work: Managing the clash of veterans, boomers, Xers, and nexters in your workplace.* New York: Amacon.
Offers insights and practical solutions for understanding differences, resolving conflicts, and managing effectively in today's age-diverse workplace. The book gives you profiles of four distinct generations, case studies in generational peace, a practice exercise, and answers to the 21 most frequently asked questions about managing in a multigenerational workplace.